C000060908

BIZARRE

TRUE CRIME

VOLUME 1

Ben Oakley

Twelvetrees Camden

Bizarre True Crime Volume 1

ISBN: 9798528198316

Independently published.

Cover design by Ulrich B.

Discover more:

www.benoakley.co.uk

"*In the end, everything is a gag.*" – Charlie Chaplin

Also by Ben Oakley

True Crime

The Monstrous Book of Serial Killers

Year of the Serial Killer Omnibus Edition

True Crime On This Day Series

The True Crime 365 series

Year of the Serial Killer Series

Harrison Lake Mysteries

Beyond the Blood Streams

Perfect Twelve

Monster of the Algarve

Honeysuckle Goodwillies

Mystery of Grimlow Forest

Subnet Series

Unknown Origin

Alien Network

Final Contact

Bizarre True Crime Volume 1

20 wacky and shocking true crime stories.

1. Ritual Murder in a Sleepy English Village

In 1945 Britain, witchcraft was long gone, but ask any local from the sleepy town of Lower Quinton, what happened to Charles Walton, and they'll tell you it was – witchcraft!

2. The Theft of Charlie Chaplin's Corpse

One of Hollywood's most famous entertainers, Charlie Chaplin, died on Christmas Day 1977. Less than three months later, his corpse was being held for ransom in a small village in Switzerland.

3. Headless Body in Topless Bar

If the New York Post's headline of 'Headless Body in Topless Bar' was written to draw you in, then the true story behind it was enough to make you vomit.

4. Keeping it in the Family

Many family discussions around the dinner table revolve around weather, news, or work. For the

Komyatti family, their discussions revolved around how to kill their father, and get away with it.

5. Lost Pirate Treasure of Captain Kidd

When two men head off on a boat, searching for the lost treasure of 17th Century pirate, Captain Kidd, they expected to find gold, but they never expected to cause an international political nightmare.

6. Visions of Murder

From a brutal murder in London to one of the most convincing cases of psychic mediumship in the history of true crime.

7. Hammer Time

An amateur playwright auditions black women for his new play, Hammer, with the intention of killing them – with a sledgehammer. On one occasion, he succeeded.

8. Body on the Highway

A pickup driver hit a woman on the highway and immediately turned himself in but an autopsy determined that the victim was already dead when the vehicle hit her!

9. Captured by his 105th Wife

The 'Pigamist' travelled the world, marrying women, then abandoning them two weeks later, after selling all of their belongings. This is the bizarre tale of how his 105th wife tracked him down.

10. Death of a Seagull

Never before had one bird caused such a flap when a professional baseball player threw a warm-up ball that struck and killed a seagull. What followed next will blow your mind!

11. Vampire of Sacramento

Richard Chase was the poster boy for bizarre serial killers whose tale included Nazi UFOs, necrophilia, cannibalism, drinking blood, and the belief he was turning to powder!

12. The Man Who Died Twice

When a fire ripped through a house in Nashville, investigators found the recently deceased body of the owner's husband, which was unusual, as the man had died ten years earlier.

13. The Haunting of Fox Hollow Farm

From a violent serial killer to a screaming ghost, the story of Herb and the haunting of Fox Hollow Farm, is one true crime tale that'll send the willies right up you!

14. The Disappearance of Bobby Dunbar

A missing boy is returned to his parents eight months after disappearing. Finally, the family can move on, except, the boy that had come back was not their son at all.

15. The Matrix Defence

A killer who brutally murdered his landlady was found not guilty as he had been sucked into the Matrix and was living in a computer-generated dream world. Yeah, this happened – twice!

16. The Shark Arm Murder Case

In Sydney, a captive tiger shark vomited a human arm, sparking an investigation that led to one of the most bizarre murder cases you'll ever read.

17. Mystery of the Body in the Tree

In 1940s England, a group of young boys were playing in the forest when they found a dead woman stuffed into the middle of a wych elm tree.

18. Factory of Death

When a Russian maniac built an underground textiles factory, he began recruiting young females, not as workers, but to fulfil his twisted dream of owning an army of slaves.

19. Great Santa Claus Robbery

The day before Christmas Eve in 1927, Santa Claus and his gang walked into a bank in Texas and robbed the joint!

20. The Fateful Story of Treaty Oak

The bizarre tale of an occultist who attempted to kill a 600-year-old victim, a tree called Treaty Oak, that owned its own land.

Ritual Murder in a Sleepy English Village

In 1945 Britain, witchcraft was long gone, but ask any local from the sleepy town of Lower Quinton, what happened to Charles Walton, and they'll tell you it was witchcraft!

Born in 1870, Charles Walton was a 74-year-old local gardener and hedge cutter who was brutally murdered on a cold Valentine's day in 1945. His body was found the same night on Firs Farm, on Meon Hill, Warwickshire. His death remains the oldest unsolved murder in Warwickshire.

Walton had been a landscaper and farm worker for most of his life, and despite walking with a stick, he was still able to take on minor jobs like hedge cutting. For nine months prior to his death, he had been working on Firs Farm, for the owner, Alfred Potter.

The day of the murder, Walton left home with his trusty pitchfork and a cutting hook and made his way to the farm. He was last seen walking past the local church at around nine in the morning. At some point during the day, Walton was brutally murdered.

Murder most horrid

Walton was living with his niece at the time of his death, Edith Walton, and she noticed he hadn't returned home at his usual time of 4pm. Due to his tendency to end up in the local pub, she dismissed it and visited her neighbour instead. By 6pm, when Walton hadn't returned, Edith and the neighbour walked over to Firs Farm and informed Alfred Potter.

Potter claimed he had last seen Walton cutting the hedges near the Hillground side of the farm, far away from the main farmhouse. The three of them traipsed over to where Walton had last been seen and stumbled upon a horrific sight.

Beside a hedgerow, hidden from view from the local lanes, was the body of Charles Walton. He had been beaten with his own stick and his neck had been cut open with the cutting hook. To top it off, the pitchfork had been driven through his neck, pinning him to the ground, and the cutting hook was left embedded in the side of his neck. A cross had been carved on his chest.

Potter, who was the only one who wasn't screaming by that point, alerted a passing local man, who in turn called the police. As the darkness set in across the hills, word was getting around Lower Quinton that old man Walton had been killed by witches.

Suspects and rumours

Professor James Webster, of the West Midlands Forensic Laboratory, arrived at the scene, hours after the police, and just before midnight. He was brought in to ascertain exactly what had happened and how many people had been involved in the murder. While he took the body away to work on it, Alfred Potter became the prime suspect.

He told police that he had been drinking at lunchtime with another farmer and had seen Walton in the Hillground cutting hedges shortly after. Due to the location the body was found at and the length of hedge that was cut, it was ascertained that Walton had been killed at approximately 2pm. Potter hadn't gone back to check on Walton as he would always make his own way home at around 4pm. On this occasion there had been a cow stuck in a ditch that required Potter's attention and he claimed he never saw Walton after that.

Before things got out of hand in the town, the local police requested the assistance of the Metropolitan Police, who were better equipped to deal with such evil. Along with witches, rumours were spreading of escaped Italian prisoners of war who were being held at a camp nearby.

Two days after the murder, Chief Inspector Robert Fabian and Detective Sergeant Albert Webb arrived in Lower Quinton. They immediately ordered a local officer to stick to Alfred Potter like glue and report back on every little thing he did.

An interpreter was sent to the Italian World War Two camp to see if the killer had come from there but reported back that every prisoner had been accounted for on the day of the murder. At the same time, Professor James Webster returned with his post-mortem results and claimed that it would have taken a man of quite some strength to have killed Walton alone.

Prime suspect

Being a farmer all his life, 40-year-old Potter would have been strong enough to overpower Walton and push the pitchfork through him. Three days after the murder, Potter was interviewed for a second time by the detectives from the Met. But already, his story wasn't matching up with the previous interview, in terms of the time he had been drinking and when he had seen Walton near the hedge.

The cow that Potter had attempted to get out of the ditch had been tested and was found to have drowned the day before the murder. The cow wasn't removed from the ditch, known as Doomsday Ditch, until 3.30pm on the 14th, approximately two hours after the murder. Potter was struggling to account for his time and Chief Inspector Fabian suspected him to be the killer.

On the 20th of February, the local officer watching Potter let slip that the forensics were taking fingerprints from the murder weapons. At which point, Potter said that he had touched the murder weapons when he first came across the body. He also strongly believed that one of the Italians had managed to escape the camp and kill Walton, calling them all the names under the Sun.

When another officer came by the farm and told them that Military Police had arrested one of the prisoners at the camp, Potter punched the air with joy and celebrated with his wife. Even though, the story of the arrest was nothing to do with the murder of Walton.

Despite the strangeness of Potter's character and version of events, no fingerprints were found on the murder weapon and he was ultimately never charged with the murder. Despite Chief Fabian being certain he was the killer, he also stated there was no evidence and no motive for Potter to have killed Walton and had mostly come across as a calm and civil man.

Enter – witchcraft!

Links to an even older murder

On a warm Autumn night in 1875, 79-year-old Ann Tennant was brutally murdered in the village of Long Compton, just fifteen miles from Lower Quinton. While returning from the shops with a loaf of bread, she passed a local farm, where a drunken local man named James Heywood was sitting.

Heywood was known to be of simple mind and a village outcast and Ann hurried past him. Another farmer nearby witnessed what happened next. Without warning, Heywood grabbed his pitchfork and attacked Ann with it. He stabbed her in the legs, head and neck, continuously stabbing her until he was restrained by the farmer and his workers.

Heywood was heard screaming that Ann was a witch, as she lay dying from her deep wounds.

He was sent to trial for murder and ultimately found not guilty on the grounds of insanity. He was sent to Broadmoor Criminal Lunatic Asylum, which still stands to this day. In an interview to discover his reasons for attacking her, he explained that Ann was one of at least 18 witches in the village and surrounding villages, and that he intended to murder every single one of them.

He refused to give the names of the other witches, in case they killed the investigators or other locals, for revealing their identity. He believed that witches had been in the village for hundreds of years and had kept their identities secret so they could live among us. He claimed to have discovered this news from a local priest, whose job it was to protect the villages.

The ghastly climax of a pagan rite

Nine years after the Walton murder, and still no closer to an arrest, the two detectives made the link between the killing of Ann Tenant and Walton. Despite being separated by 70 years, the two murders were remarkably similar. A closer inspection revealed that Tennant had a cutting hook embedded into her neck, the same as Walton.

The detectives discovered that the method of murder, using the cutting hook and pitchfork, was an Anglo-Saxon method of killing witches. At around the same time, the Met were provided with evidence and material that has since never been released to the public. Leading to further speculation of something mysterious going on in Lower Quinton.

Chief Inspector Fabian later left the investigation unsolved, stating they had done all they could for the local police. As the years went by, when asked about the case, he had one final message for anyone looking into it.

"I advise anybody who is tempted at any time to venture into Black Magic, witchcraft, Shamanism – call it what you will – to remember Charles Walton and to think of his death, which was clearly the ghastly climax of a pagan rite. There is no stronger argument for keeping as far away as possible from the villains with their swords, incense and mumbo-jumbo. It is prudence on which your future peace of mind and even your life could depend." Chief Inspector Fabian, many years after the Walton murder.

The Quinton Witch

What happened to Chief Inspector Fabian to have him leave the investigation? What material did he and his colleagues uncover? Did they discover evidence of a witch in the small English village? Over the years, many investigations have taken place and many theories have been put forward, all backed up with tons of supposed evidence, but the most common one is the following.

Charles Walton's great-grandparents were Thomas Walton and Ann Smith. Smith was Ann Tennant's maiden name, born in 1794. She gave birth to William Walton who was Charles Walton's grandfather. When Thomas died of illness five years later, she remarried John Tennant in 1819. This led some to believe that Ann Tennant was the great-grandmother of Charles Walton.

What does this have to do with Charles' murder?

An old book about folklore written by a local priest had been sent to Chief Inspector Fabian from another officer. In it, there is a story regarding Charles Walton. In 1885, a young plough boy named Charles Walton was walking home from work at a farm when he encountered a ghostly black dog. This happened for three nights in a row until the last night when the dog was accompanied by a headless woman. On the last night, Walton's sister mysteriously died.

To the locals this was proof that Charles Walton was a witch and was even feared by some villagers. It was one of the reasons why he kept himself to himself. Locals later claimed he could cast evil spells and kept toads as pets, which were used to kill farmers crops. He was even said to have been involved in the death of Potter's cow, the night before his death.

Locals banded together and murdered Walton using an ancient ritual so that his blood could soak into the ground to replenish the land. Shortly after Walton was murdered, locals reported seeing black dogs on the field and on the lanes around the village.

If Charles Winton was a witch, then it stands to some bizarre reason that his great-grandmother was too. And so, if James Heywood is to be believed that there were 18 witches in the Warwickshire villages at the time of Ann's death, then Charles would have been the second. Only 16 witches to go.

Despite the tales of witchcraft, what we do know is that Charles Walton was murdered in a ritualistic fashion in a small English village, and the case has never been solved.

The Theft of Charlie Chaplin's Corpse

One of Hollywood's most famous entertainers, Charlie Chaplin, died on Christmas Day 1977. Less than three months later, his corpse was being held for ransom in a small village in Switzerland.

There is a strange and unusual history of people profiteering from human remains, with corpse kidnapping being at the top of the list.

From archaeological grave robbers to Victorian body snatchers, making money from the dead has been with us for a long time. There was even a plot to get hold of Abraham Lincoln's body shortly after his assassination in order to hold it for ransom. It didn't work, nor did the Chaplin plan.

In Lake Geneva, Switzerland, two mechanics named Roman Wardas and Gantscho Ganev came up with a brilliant, fool-proof plan to make a load of money. The plan was simple, dig up the body of Charlie Chaplin, hide the corpse, and send his widow a ransom note, which she'd surely pay.

What follows is the story of the most spectacularly unsuccessful cases of graverobbing in modern history.

The Chaplin plan

Roman was a 24-year-old Polish refugee who was in financial ruin, running away from multiple problems and struggling to survive. He had followed the story of Chaplin's death, and more importantly where he had been buried.

Chaplin had lived out the rest of his days in Switzerland, near Lake Geneva, in the village of Corsier-sur-Vevey. He had retired from Hollywood with his fourth wife, Oona Chaplin, who was 36 years his junior. They had married when Oona was 18 and

Charlie was 56, warranting a story by itself. Chaplin died aged 88-years-old.

Inspired by a similar story that had happened in Italy, Roman believed his plan was fool-proof but he needed a second pair of hands. Enter Gantscho, a 38-year-old Bulgarian national who had been struggling to find employment since arriving in Switzerland. After a night of drinking, Roman managed to convince Gantscho to join him in his crazy plan.

Digging up the body

In the middle of the night on 1st March 1978, Roman and Gantscho crept into the Corsier cemetery, with shovels in hand. They found Chaplin's headstone and began digging for the next two hours, until they could drag the coffin from its pitch.

Between the two of them, they managed to lift the heavy wooden coffin into Ganev's car. They drove to a nearby cornfield and dug another hole. Satisfied the hole was deep enough, they lowered the coffin in and filled in the hole.

Roman later claimed the second hole was not going to be needed because the plan was to have a bizarre twist in its tail. The pair had no intention of moving the coffin in a vehicle as they weren't going to move it at all. Instead, Roman's plan was to dig beneath the coffin and bury it deeper in the same location, then put a top layer of soil on, and make it look as though the coffin had been moved.

Due to heavy rain the night before, the earth around the coffin had become too heavy and they decided to bury it at another location. Which meant Chaplin's body had a tour of his retirement village from the back seats of an old mechanic's car.

The ransom call, and note, and begging.

The following day, Gantscho went off to look for work, while Roman put the rest of his plan into action but not before the police beat him to it. While finishing up breakfast, Oona Chaplin got a call from the Swiss police with some unusual news.

"*Look*," they had said, "*somebody dug up the grave and he's gone.*"

Somehow, Oona was unperturbed by the news and thought the whole thing rather ridiculous, until Roman called.

Roman, who was pretending to be a man named 'Mr. Rochat', phoned in the ransom and demanded the equivalent of $600,000 (USD)/£400,000 (GBP). Oona, still believing the whole situation to be ridiculous, hung up and ignored him, refusing to pay anything.

In the days that followed, news got around the village that Charlie Chaplin's coffin was missing. Soon, Hollywood and international media had got hold of the story. Oona and the family kept quiet about the ransom demands, which led the media to creating their own stories surrounding the mystery.

One Hollywood report claimed the coffin had been dug up because Chaplin was a Jew and the cemetery was non-Jewish. Another that the Chaplin family wanted him buried in a more agreeable location, none of which were true. Seeing the unexpected media attention over the story, Roman began threatening the Chaplin family to force them to pay up.

Oona later said in an interview that she found the whole situation rather funny and that '*Charlie would have thought it rather ridiculous.*'

Disturbing the peace of the dead

Despite the intense media coverage over the missing body, Roman never gave up. He phoned and wrote ransom notes constantly, almost begging to be paid, not that he had worked out how he was going to collect the money. He had even resorted to threatening Chaplin's younger children.

An estimated 27 ransom calls were made from the two mechanics to the police or the Chaplin residence. Police tapped Oona's phoneline and had detectives and officers monitoring every single one of the region's two hundred phone booths.

Ten weeks later, on 16th May 1978, police traced the latest call to a phone booth near Corsier, and arrested both Roman and Gantscho, who were loitering nearby. The arrests put to bed one of Lake Geneva's largest crime stories for many years.

Both men led investigators to the cornfield where they had buried the coffin in a shallow grave. In December

1978, both men were convicted of extortion and disturbing the peace of the dead. Roman was sentenced to four-and-a-half years of hard labour, and Gantscho was given an 18-month suspended sentence due to limited responsibility for the crime.

In later years, Eugene Chaplin, Charlie's son, claimed that both of the graverobbers wrote letters to Oona, expressing their regret. One simply said, '*we're so sorry.*'

Chaplin was ultimately reburied in the same plot he had been taken from, in Corsier cemetery. Except, this time, the coffin was buried in concrete, to deter any other masterminds planning to hold Charlie's corpse for ransom. Oona was buried next to her husband after her death in 1991.

"In the end, everything is a gag." – Charlie Chaplin

Headless Body in Topless Bar

If the New York Post's headline of 'Headless Body in Topless Bar' was written to draw you in, then the true story behind it was enough to make you vomit.

Throughout history, there has been an abundance of memorable newspaper headlines. The British tabloid, The Daily Mirror, had '*Die, You Bastard*' in relation to sex killer Ian Huntley when he was suffering from an illness. God bless them.

But perhaps no more fitting, yet undeniably gruesome headline, has had a longer lasting impression on those who read it than the New York Post's '*Headless Body in Topless Bar*'.

The strip joint

When he was in his late teens, New York born Charles Dingle dreamed of being an officer of the law. In his early Twenties, he applied to the force but was ultimately rejected due to his growing criminal record, most of which included drug offences. He ultimately settled on becoming a security guard, the only job he could get that vaguely resembled an officer.

When he was only 23-years-old, Dingle got high on drink and drugs, including cocaine, and ventured down to a strip joint called Herbies Bar, owned by 51-year-old local businessman Herbert Cummings. The bar, located in Queens, had no dancers up on the podiums as it was a night when they weren't scheduled to dance.

Immediately, this had enraged Dingle and he began shouting at Herbert to get some of the girls up and dancing. Herbert's wife, who was one of the strippers, sat next to Dingle to try and calm him down. Dingle then drank enough booze to sink the titanic and began snorting lines of coke off the bar in full view of the other patrons.

Later that night, when Dingle was handed his bill, he refused to pay and again argued with Herbert. During the argument, some of the remaining customers left, leaving four strippers and Herbert behind. He ordered Dingle to leave the premises but Dingle responded by pulling a gun from his jacket and shooting Herbert in the head at point blank range, killing him instantly.

The madman

In a blind rage, Dingle locked the doors to the bar and held the four female strippers' hostage, threatening them with a bullet to the head if they screamed. Realising he had nowhere to go, he dragged one of the strippers to a table near the bar, tore off her clothing and raped her in front of the other three women.

Just as he was about to continue with the next victim, there was a knock at the door. One of Herbert's female friends was outside, supposedly to meet him when the bar closed. Dingle forced her inside the bar at gunpoint and threw her to the floor. When he went through her purse he found a business card that said the woman was a mortician.

Suddenly, a light bulb went off in his demented head. He came up with a plan he believed would absolve him of responsibility of the shooting. He needed to get the bullet out of Herbert's head. He gave the woman a small steak knife and ordered her to dig the bullet out so police wouldn't be able to link his gun to the slaying.

Forced at gunpoint, the woman did as she was told, digging into Herbert's skull to remove the bullet but she didn't have the right tools for the job. Instead, Dingle ordered her to cut off Herbert's head. Despite trying to escape, the mortician had no choice and got to work, decapitating Herbert in front of the four strippers, one of whom was Herbert's wife.

Head in a box

The scene in the strip joint was as horrific as you could have imagined. The strippers were cowering in the corner of the bar, afraid what the drugged-up Dingle was going to do next. Their boss's bloodied and headless body was at the far side of the bar, and Dingle was carefully placing the head in a box.

But not just any box, Dingle had gone out of his way to dress the box with decorations and streamers, in a sick attempt to hide what was really inside. He then called a taxi, and when it arrived, he ordered the driver into the bar at gunpoint. Dingle then kidnapped the mortician and Herbert's wife and drove over to Manhattan in the stolen taxi.

His plan was to throw the head into the river and then rape both women. Yet, the vast amount of booze and drugs he had consumed were taking hold of him and he started passing out. Before long, the car was parked on Broadway at West 168th Street, and Dingle was fast asleep in the front seat. Seeing an opportunity, the mortician and Herbert's wife escaped and rushed to the police.

Police officers descended on the vehicle and dragged Dingle out of the seat while he was still asleep. He woke up pretty sharpish after that and fought with five officers who managed to subdue him. On the passenger seat was the box with Herbert's head inside.

Dingle was convicted of murder, kidnapping, rape and robbery, he was sentenced to 25-years to life in prison. Since his conviction, Dingle has repeatedly assaulted prison staff and tried to conceal deadly weapons, including a shank. He has been denied parole at every opportunity and remains in prison to this day.

Keeping it in the Family

Many family discussions around the dinner table revolve around weather, news, or work. For the Komyatti family, their discussions revolved around how to kill their father, and get away with it.

Conversations of murder

An entire family colluded to murder their 62-year-old family member. After multiple failed attempts, they succeeded and cut up his body while joking about their various failed attempts.

On 20th March 1983, 62-year-old Paul Komyatti Sr. was stabbed to death and dismembered by his son-in-law William E. Vandiver, his son Paul Komyatti Jr, his daughter Mariann Vandiver, and his wife, Rosemary.

A month before the murder, Mariann was staying at her parent's home with her grandson, Jason, as she and Vandiver were having money troubles and were supposedly on the run from Chicago police. If Mariann ever had a choice, it would not have been to go back home. Her memories of childhood were far from peaceful.

Paul Jr. was beaten so badly by his father as a child that he developed a stutter. Rosemary would take him and run away to her sister's home. But Paul Sr. would always come after them, coercing them back. There were even occasions where Paul Sr. would stick a gun to the side of his son's head and threaten to shoot him unless his mother returned home to him.

Paul Sr. was known to have been a loud and violent drunk who was hated by members of his immediate family. He was domineering to his wife and strict to his children, who despised the ground he walked on. He had ordered his daughter multiple times to divorce Vandiver because of previous criminal activity but the order was not taken too well.

One night, while their father was asleep, Paul Jr. and Mariann discussed the possibility of killing their father. Surprisingly, the conversation went well and they both agreed that it was the best thing for everyone. They approached their mother Rosemary who literally had no objections to killing him, but with one stipulation, it had to be done away from the house to hide any evidence.

To facilitate the conversations about murder, Mariann moved into a friend's house with Vandiver, and the residence became the planning headquarters for the murder of Paul Sr. Her friend was rarely at home which made the property a perfect den for murder talk.

Failed attempts at murder

One has to wonder how a conversation like that goes. They would have had to look at the repercussions and every possible outcome regarding the murder. In fact, it wasn't only one plan they came up with, it was multiple plans, because every time they tried to secretly kill him, the hardy construction worker survived.

The first murder plot was to shoot him as he left a bar and rob him of his belongings to make it look like a robbery. However, no one owned a gun except for Vandiver, and he refused point blank to take an action so bold and in the open, with possible witnesses all over the place.

The next idea was to poison him. Rosemary, who worked at a pharmacy, managed to get hold of some nitroglycerine, which was known to decrease blood flow to the heart and cause heart attacks. The family substituted Paul's medication with the drug and sat back in the hopes he would just keel over and die.

It didn't work, instead, Rosemary had to report back to HQ that he had nausea, dizziness, vomiting, and headaches, but was still alive. Paul Jr. then purchased some rat poison, and he and Vandiver went about moulding the poison to look like the medication. Again, they sat back and waited in the hope that he would simply die. They continued with the rat poison for a number of days before Paul Sr. suggested he go to the doctors as he was constantly feeling ill. You guessed it, he didn't die.

Aggrieved at the situation and worried a doctor would discover traces of rat poison, they changed methods and got hold of some liquid poison from a black market seller. Rosemary purchased a syringe and secretly poisoned Paul's coffee a number of times but – you guessed it, he didn't die.

Getting desperate, the family plotters got hold of some more nitroglycerine and switched out the medication again. Before Paul Sr. could take it, he become ill over dinner and retreated to the bedroom. Then another discussion took place.

After various failed poisonings and murder plots, the family and Vandiver came up with a fool-proof idea; knock him out and inject air bubbles into his veins. Vandiver decided that Rosemary should use ether to render Paul unconscious and then he and Paul Jr. would use the syringe to inject air bubbles into him.

Joking about dismemberment

The plan was thrown out because Mariann walked out and left for Georgia, deciding she would have no further part in the plot to kill her father. The following day, Paul Sr. was becoming irate as he was beginning to suspect something was amiss in the house of Komyatti. He threatened Rosemary and claimed he was going to go through her credit card purchases and receipts to find out what she had been buying.

Rosemary called Mariann and Vandiver, who returned to the home one last time. They all agreed that something needed to be done immediately, as Paul Sr. was becoming more violent with each passing hour, even threatening to beat Rosemary with a belt and disrupt her place of work. The family plotters decided to go with the injection of air plan and put it into action in the early hours of the morning on 20th March 1983.

Vandiver and Paul Jr. crept into the bedroom of Paul Sr. and attempted to knock him out with the ether. But Paul Sr. was too strong and he fought back with all his might. Vandiver attempted to knock him out with the butt of his gun but it didn't work. Instead, Vandiver ordered Paul Jr. to hold his father's legs down. Vandiver then stabbed Paul Sr. with a fish knife – over 100 times.

When they returned to the living room, where Rosemary and Mariann were waiting, they had to explain that it didn't quite go to plan, and now the bedroom was covered in blood. When they all returned to the bedroom, Vandiver believed he heard Paul Sr.

still breathing and proceeded to cut off his head to confirm the kill.

A couple of hours later, the four of them used various instruments to dissect the body and place small parts into various garbage bags they intended to dump in the river. They joked about the various failed methods they had used and how they were finally free of the drunken Paul Sr. It was, if you could imagine, a perfect family conversation.

Vandiver offered the dead man's penis to Rosemary as a joke. They all laughed at the toughness of the skin and flesh. Vandiver had to teach Paul Jr. how to dissect with the knife because the saw was jamming up with pieces of fat and flesh. There was even a joke about how his heart looked like a chicken heart, with the amount of fat around it. They all took smoke breaks because of the smell and the time it was taking to cut up the remains.

Dumping the body parts – badly

They spent an hour placing various body parts into the bags, along with other evidence of the crime. Rosemary and Mariann helped dispose of the clothing and bedsheets and cleaned down the bedroom. While Paul Jr. and Vandiver drove a long length of Lake Michigan, disposing of the bags at various intervals.

A short while later, having not weighed down the bags heavily enough, the body parts began washing up on the shores of the Lake. An investigation led to the family and all four were arrested for conspiracy to murder.

Surprisingly, Vandiver admitted what had happened immediately, stating that he saw no sense in wasting everybody's time. At the same time, Rosemary, Mariann, and Paul Jr. turned on Vandiver during the investigation period, and claimed he had been responsible for everything that had happened. You have to wonder, if it had been a secret conversation between the three should things have gone tits up, like they did.

At trial, Vandiver recanted his confessions and placed the entire blame on Paul Jr. for the murder and dissection. Still, the jury and judge saw the truth of what happened and all four were convicted for the brutal murder of Paul Sr.

Vandiver was sentenced to death and executed in the electric chair in Indiana on 16th October 1985. At his execution, the current had to be applied three times before he died. Escaping the death penalty through testimony, Paul Jr. was sentenced to 100 years in prison, 55 for murder, and 45 for conspiracy to commit murder. He was released on parole in 2010 for good behaviour credits.

Rosemary was sentenced to the same tariff of 100 years. An appeal for her release was rejected in 2010 and she was due to be released in 2033. Mariann escaped with the lighter sentence of eight years, since she testified against her family, and was the one who wanted minimal part in the crime.

A local paper at the time wrote, 'the only relative in the house who wasn't plotting Paul Komyatti's murder in Hammond last winter was his 5-year-old grandson.'

Lost Pirate Treasure of Captain Kidd

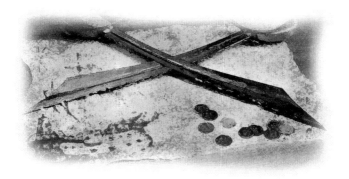

When two men head off on a boat, searching for the lost treasure of 17th Century pirate, Captain Kidd, they expected to find gold, but they never expected to cause an international political nightmare.

On a murky night in Pattaya, Thailand, in the Summer of 1983, two men crossed paths that led them on a bizarre mission. 47-year-old failed British comedian Richard Knight was sitting at a bar scouring local maps, when he was joined by 18-year-old American Cork Graham, fresh out of high school.

Cork was a combat photographer who had been involved in the Kampuchea/Vietnam War and Hmong resistance in Laos. He was on a mission to discover what had happened to Americans who were listed as Missing in Action, and whether they had passed on or fled to a new life. While researching, he accepted Knight's invitation to join him on a treasure hunting expedition.

Unfortunately, it meant getting close to the ocean border of Vietnam, which was off-limits to Westerners in the Eighties. Maybe a little too close, in fact, they went straight over the border and illegally entered Vietnam. Shortly after, they were attacked by Vietnamese officials, accused of being spies, and held as political prisoners.

Pirate treasure map mystery

Knight claimed he was in possession of a map passed down from his grandfather that showed where Captain Kidd's treasure was buried. It was a 300-year-old map that seemed unlikely to have pointed to where Captain Kidd and his ship, the Adventure Galley, buried their hauls. However, Knight was adamant the treasure was there.

After studying maps and charts drawn by the pirate, he became convinced the bounty was buried on the small Vietnamese island of Hon Tre Lon, despite many other treasure hunters looking nearer the Caribbean.

Cork on the other hand was unsure the treasure existed but even if it didn't, being invited on a treasure hunt was too enticing to pass over. They rented a speedboat with two Thai boatmen the next morning and set sail from the Pattaya shoreline, armed with an old treasure map and a belief they could find something.

The waters around Pattaya and onward to the Vietnam shoreline is littered with smaller islands and places where it did seem likely that pirate ships may have ventured all those years ago. However, their expedition was cut short, when on 17th June, they were arrested by Vietnamese authorities who had seen their boat on the shore.

Knight and Cork were charged with illegally entering Vietnam and were accused of being spies. They were taken to a provincial prison in Kien Giang and held prisoner until a makeshift trial could begin. The two boatmen were detained at the same prison.

Tortured and convicted

Meanwhile, in Hanoi, a Western official who was aware the two men had been arrested was following the case closely. He was able to locate the pair one month later in the prison and informed their families. But the Vietnamese denied even detaining the men until international pressure began to mount.

Both men were interrogated and tortured for the next couple of months, with mock executions and sleep deprivation. Finally, in September of 1983, four months after their arrest, the Vietnamese contacted the British Government to inform them they were holding Knight and Cork.

Two months after that, the men were found guilty of illegally entering Vietnam and giving a $10,000 fine, which if it were paid, they could be released. The families of both men could not afford the fines and appealed for their release on humanitarian grounds.

The Vietnamese stood by the court's ruling and expected the British and American authorities to pay the fines, in order to release the prisoners. Before Cork and Knight knew what was going on, the fine had become a ransom.

In the late Winter, Cork and Knight were transferred to an old French military compound in Ho Chi Minh City. There, they were given a balanced diet but kept locked in a small room together, getting minimal light and outside exercise. Both men had begun suffering from illness and depression.

The charitable adventurer

In May of 1984, Cork's family had raised the money needed to pay the fine and release him. Cork was released shortly after and flown home to be the focus of international media. Meanwhile, back in the old French compound, Knight remained. His family could only manage to raise a fifth of the fine and the Vietnamese refused to let him go.

Enter British adventurer and businessman Kenneth Crutchlow. He had read about the capture and detainment of the two men, along with the release of Cork, and was aggrieved that the British Government wouldn't help out one of their own. Truth was that both the British and American Governments didn't pay the fine as it may have set a precedent for future cases.

Crutchlow had just set up a taxicab firm and used some of the profit from it to pay the fine. After a lengthy back-and-forth with the Vietnamese authorities, Crutchlow donated $8,000, on top of Knight's family efforts of $2,000. In August of 1984, Knight was flown home to his family, but was suffering from severe depression due to his detainment.

But Crutchlow wasn't finished, the two Thai boatmen who had taken Cork and Knight out onto the waters, were still being held captive. He stated in a later interview that it was an Englishman who got them into Vietnam, and it would be an Englishman who got them out. He felt it was his duty as an Englishman to do what he could.

44 months later, after selling part of his taxi firm, Crutchlow was able to pay the boatmen's bail to the Vietnamese embassy in Bangkok. The men were released shortly after and flown back to Thailand. Crutchlow was also known for founding the Ocean Rowing Society International (ORSI). He died of natural causes in 2016.

Richard Knight's memoirs were later written by Glenys Roberts. In the memoirs, Knight explains that they had found part of the treasure on the island and reburied it before they were arrested by the Vietnamese. Before he could return to Vietnam to dig up the loot, Knight passed away, taking the location of the buried treasure to his grave, just as Captain Kidd did.

A diplomat later called the treasure hunt a fruitless exercise, as no historian could agree on whether Captain Kidd and the Adventure Galley had ever sailed in waters near the islands. Despite this, there was a theory that the Vietnamese were protecting its true location, as they searched for it themselves, along with Knight's map.

Perhaps the treasure of Captain Kidd did exist after all.

Visions of Murder

From a brutal murder in London to one of the most convincing cases of psychic mediumship in the history of true crime.

On a cold London night in February 1983, 25-year-old Jaqueline Poole was raped, beaten, and strangled to death. The barmaid from Ruislip was living alone at the time and was due at work the next day.

When her family failed to contact her, the father of her boyfriend visited the home and became concerned for her wellbeing. He managed to enter the property through the living room window and was met with the gruesome sight of Poole's lifeless and brutalised body.

The media latched onto the story and murder was splashed all over the local newspapers but not many details of the crime were released. Detectives wanted to keep the details of the crime secret so that it could aid in their investigation.

One day after the murder, a young woman by the name of Christine Holohan, who was studying to become a professional medium, had a vision. Aged 22, she dreamt of a young woman named Jackie Hunt, who had been murdered in the most horrific of ways.

The following morning, she went to the police and described her vision to them. The police were shocked because Christine had given them Jaqueline Poole's maiden name, which was Hunt, a detail that hadn't been released to the public.

Christine told police that Jaqueline called in sick to work and was later visited by a shady man who she let into her apartment. She had apparently known the man but didn't really like him. As the evening continued, the man became violent and attacked her, brutally killing her with his bare hands.

Now, if you're thinking this all sounds like gobbledegook, then you might be right. But Christine was able to describe the murder scene in such detail that the leading detective believed everything she said. It took 18 years for science to catch up with Christine's testimony, at last giving the DNA evidence needed to convict the killer.

Psychic Witness

She met with Detective Andrew Smith and Officer Tony Batters, and recounted the story that the vision had shown her. Though few details were released at the time, Holohan was able to list over 100 distinct details of the crime scene, none of which had been made public and were only known to the investigatory team.

Though the body was found on the living room floor, the attack had started in the bathroom, where Jaqueline had been trying to lock herself in. Christine told them the attack had started in the bathroom, another detail that was never released to the public.

Christine described the number of cushions there were and their exact positions, along with how the furniture had been moved around. She described how Jaqueline had changed clothes multiple times during the day and which newspapers were dotted around the home. She could even tell them how much coffee had been left in the cups.

After her description of the crime scene and the details of the murder, the detectives turned to her description of the killer. After allowing Christine to enter a trance-like state, she began talking about the killer.

The murderer

Jaqueline's ex-husband was in jail at the time of the murder but she would visit him on a regular basis, the most recent being two weeks before her death. Christine claimed that the prison, she referred to in the British slang term of 'nick', was the connection to the killer. Both Jaqueline and her husband knew the killer and Christine referred to the mystery killer as the 'bird'.

In her trance, Christine relayed the following information. The killer was five-foot eight, dark skin, wavy hair, in his early Twenties. He had arm tattoos of a sword, snake, or rose, and was a Taurus, born in the months of April or May. She even went as far as giving a name to the killer; Tony. But Tony went by a nickname called 'Pokie'.

She claimed the killer worked as a painter or some other profession that required him to use a brush, and that he had robbed people's homes in the past. With regards to the theft of jewellery from Jaqueline's home, Christine gave them the number of 221.

The officers learned that a nearby road had house numbers going up to 221. When they searched the nearby park, they found a small rock formation that covered a hole, a perfect place to hide the goods, which were missing. It was suspected the killer had buried the jewellery then returned later to collect them.

Despite the clues that Holohan was able to provide the police, the killer wasn't found at the time, but his DNA was kept on record for such a time when it could be used. It turns out, the investigation had to wait 18 years for Christine to be proven right.

Time's up!

In 2001, Anthony Ruark was arrested for Jaqueline's murder. He was arrested for theft just one year earlier and his DNA had been secured as part of the arrest. When the DNA was checked against the database, it was a match for some of the skin that was found underneath Jaqueline's fingernails. The killer had been caught and his time on the run was up.

Police went back and matched Christine's details with Ruark. He was five-foot nine of mixed race, and was born in late April, a Taurus. He was 23-years-old at the time of the murder, had many tattoos all over his body, and was a part time plasterer. He made most of his money robbing houses and stealing cars. More importantly, Tony was short for Anthony, and his was known by the nickname; Pokie.

With DNA evidence secured, along with Christine's testimony from the original investigation, Ruark was convicted of Jaqueline's rape, robbery, and murder, and sentenced to life in prison.

The details that Christine had given the original investigation were considered so good that it remains one of the most convincing cases of psychic mediumship in the history of crime.

Hammer Time

An amateur playwright auditions black women for his new play, Hammer, with the intention of killing them – with a sledgehammer. On one occasion, he succeeded.

Aspiring actress, 20-year-old Patricia Cowan, was browsing the adverts at the back of a local newspaper when she came across the one she was looking for. A Detroit playwright was looking for a black actress to audition for a play called Hammer.

The audition had originally been given to Brenda Murray Starr, who worked with Patricia in an amateur troupe called Detroit's Finest Love Theatrical Company. She turned down the offer of reading for the play and mentioned it in passing to Patricia, showing her the newspaper advert.

Excited, Patricia jumped at the opportunity and made the phone call to the young black man who had placed the advert. She asked if she could bring her four-year-old son, Dequan, with her, as she couldn't get a sitter in time. The playwright agreed and offered her $100 to read the part for him in his garage the following day.

Except, the playwright, 21-year-old James Thomas, had a quite different reason for inviting her to his garage. James had set up the audition so that he could kill a black female. Despite being black himself, he had an underlying hatred of black women but never gave any other motive for what he did next.

The audition

On Sunday 9th April 1978, Patricia and her son arrived at James' garage to find three additional people inside. James' girlfriend, and two unidentified men were waiting for her. Their belief was that they would listen to the reading and help James decide.

During the reading, Patricia was playing as the wife of James' character. They were acting out a scene together where the married couple were arguing and the reading was said to have become heated. At the height of the argument, James grabbed his five-pound sledgehammer from the side of the garage and slammed it into the actress's head.

Later, at the trial, James claimed he suddenly blacked out and had no idea what he was doing, having no memory of the incident. Despite that, as Patricia had fallen to the ground, he hit her several more times. At some point, he hit four-year-old Dequan with the hammer.

The hammer killer

Patricia's body and her son were dumped in an alleyway just four blocks from the garage. That night, a group of boys skateboarding nearby heard a child screaming. They ventured into the alley and stumbled on the horrific scene in front of them.

Detective Peter Keliher was put on the case and discovered that Dequan had survived the attack but was left with life-changing injuries. The investigation traced Patricia's friend, Brenda, who told them of the audition and the connection to James was made immediately.

James, his girlfriend, and the two never-identified men were arrested and brought in for questioning. His girlfriend and the other two men were not involved but had watched the attack in horror. It remained unclear if they had known about James's intentions beforehand.

James confessed to the murder, despite his amnesia, and pleaded guilty at a subsequent trial. He was convicted of second-degree murder and assault with intent to murder. He was ultimately sentenced to two full life terms and was never released from prison.

Due to claiming he had blacked out, James has never given a motive for the murder but he was known to have a hatred for black women. With that being his only tentative motive, it has long been believed that he had written Hammer with the sole intention of killing a black female with a hammer.

The play itself has never been released to the public. We are only left to imagine the final scene.

Body on the Highway

A pickup driver hit a woman on the highway and immediately turned himself in but an autopsy determined that the victim was already dead when the vehicle hit her!

In the early hours of the morning during a cold March in 1978, Charles Clark was driving his pickup truck home along a local highway. He quickly became distracted by a speeding car behind him with full headlights and the car passed him, barely missing the pickup. As Clark checked his speedometer to look at his own speed, he hit something in the road and the car bounced to a halt.

In the passing car, a young couple on their way home were having fun and talking about their night when they noticed the truck they'd just passed bounce over something. Both vehicles stopped to see what had happened. In the middle of the road, a few metres behind Clark's truck, was the mangled body of 29-year-old Wanda Pearl Murray.

Clark called the police and informed them that he was distracted and hadn't seen Wanda walking into the road. Unbeknownst to Clark at the time, Wanda wasn't walking at all, in fact, she was already dead.

Short-lived homicide investigation

Clark passed a breathalyser test at the scene and was cleared of any wrongdoing. However, there was a strong smell of alcohol on the road. The alcohol smell was coming from Wanda's blood and her internal organs which were strewed across the width of the highway. Initially, investigators assumed she had been drunk and walked into the path of Clark's vehicle by accident.

When the on-site coroner returned with his report, it appeared something was amiss. Though there was a lot of blood at the scene and Wanda's organs were severely damaged, consistent with being hit by a car, there was no blood from wounds that had bled. This meant that the car had hit Wanda after her death and he recommended a homicide investigation.

Wanda was a divorced mother of two who had been out drinking with her boyfriend the night of her death and the investigation delved deeper. Her ex-husband had custody of their children due to her record of shoplifting and otherwise unsavoury behaviour.

She was being sponsored by a local priest and his family but despite the assistance she was getting to better her life, she was unable to find a job and her life began to deteriorate. Wanda found solace in alcohol and spent most of her nights drinking in local bars which led to violent behaviour, at which point the priest and his family asked her to leave their home.

She moved in with her boyfriend, Airforce Lieutenant Luther Brown, who was living in a military residence. He told investigators that he had once called Military Police to his apartment as Wanda's mood swings had become too much for him to handle.

At that point, Brown became a suspect in Wanda's death, as investigators believed Wanda's body had been thrown out of a car at high speed, probably by a man with some strength. But Brown claimed he had split up with Wanda and asked her to leave a few nights before her death. The security at the base confirmed that Brown was in his apartment at the time of Wanda's death.

The investigation turned to Wanda's schedule on the evening before.

A mysterious well-dressed man

Brown told investigators to talk to her friends, who were better placed to know what she was up to at any given moment. One of her friends, Dee Smith, told them that Wanda was out drinking with another friend named Faye, at a local bar the night of Wanda's death. Faye was drinking in an attempt to take her mind off her violent ex-boyfriend, Kevin Milroy.

Kevin just so happened to track Faye down to the bar and became violent with her in front of other patrons. Wanda attacked Kevin to protect her friend, but Kevin was heard threatening to kill her for interfering with their relationship. Later that night, Faye and Kevin were seen arguing outside the bar, and the bouncer, who was Military Police by day, ordered them to leave.

Immediately, Kevin became the prime suspect but then the bartenders told a different story. After Kevin and Faye left the premises, Wanda was seen drinking heavily with an unidentified man who appeared to be well-dressed and much older than her. They were seen chatting and drinking until the bar closed just before two in the morning.

One of the bartenders was checking the outside of the bar when he saw Wanda staggering around and asked her to pay for her last drink. She ignored him and staggered over to a car where the well-dressed man was waiting. She fell into the passenger seat and the man drove away.

The time between Wanda leaving with the man and then dying, was too little to believe anyone else was a suspect. The investigation focused heavily on finding the man but just as they were to start searching for the suspected killer, an astonishing revelation came back from the coroner.

One final twist

The coroner had run Wanda's blood through the system and the toxicology report had just come back. He couldn't believe what he was looking at. Wanda was a diabetic, which wasn't uncommon, except she didn't know she was diabetic.

Due to the amount of alcohol she had been drinking in the weeks leading up to her death and the large amount of alcohol in the hours before, the coroner believed the alcohol had killed her. He explained that her body was unable to cope with the high level of consumption and he concluded that it had caused hyperglycaemia, or high blood glucose.

This level of alcohol would have put Wanda into a diabetic coma. Her organs would have shut down, almost immediately, and her breathing would have slowed and then ultimately stopped. It had also gone some way to explain her violent and panicky behaviour when drunk.

Armed with this new information, the investigators suspected that the well-dressed man was driving to his home when he realised Wanda had died on the seat next to him. In a panic, he opened the door and pushed her body into the road, before speeding away. A few minutes later, Charles Clark hit her body in his pickup truck.

Regarding the well-dressed man, the investigation decided not to pursue him for abusing a corpse due to lack of funds and resources. The mystery man might not ever know that he was once the prime suspect in the death of girl who had already died.

Captured By His 105th Wife

The 'Pigamist' travelled the world, marrying women, then abandoning them two weeks later, after selling all of their belongings. This is the bizarre tale of how his 105th wife tracked him down.

In Mesa, Arizona, in the hot Spring of 1981, 43-year-old real estate agent Patricia Ann Gardiner had found herself smitten with the man of her dreams. He was confident, smart, and wooed her with gifts and declarations of love. Before she knew it, she was on a whirlwind romance and was married quicker than she knew what was going on.

That man was Giovanni Vigliotto, who by his claim would marry 105 women across the world, though some suggested it was only 83. Despite this, Patricia had no idea of Giovanni's reckless bigamy and gave him the keys to her life – and personal belongings.

One day, when Patricia was out the house, Giovanni loaded all of her possessions into a moving van and then drove off. Giovanni never returned, and he had no intention of doing so. He sold all of her possessions at local flea markets and cleaned out her bank accounts, making off with at least $36,000 in cash. This was two weeks after they had married.

At first, Patricia was shocked but then it dawned on her exactly what was going on – she had been conned. She claimed the romance was quick and the courtship short and she had made an impulsive decision to marry him due to his unseen manipulation of her. It was then, she decided to give chase.

Tracking the Pigamist

Unlike many of his previous victims, Patricia had quickly come to terms with the fact she had been conned. The swiftness of her decision-making after

Giovanni had left, would be responsible for bringing him to justice.

She contacted the police and told them what had happened, even describing the direction he may have driven off in. Investigators linked with nearby States and connected various reports from previous years about a man who had quickly married only to run off with his new wife's possessions.

But Patricia was concerned there had been so many reports with no arrest and took matters into her own hands. Armed with the little knowledge she had from other investigations and an approximate direction Giovanni had headed in, she gave chase.

Over the coming months, she managed to track Giovanni's movements from Arizona and onto the East coast of the country. As she had met him at a flea market, she went to all the flea markets she could find along the Eastern routes. In fact, Patricia hunted him down over 2,000 miles to Florida where she finally caught a break, six months after he had vanished.

She spotted Giovanni selling her possessions in Panama City and immediately contacted the police. Much to her delight – and his shock – Giovanni was arrested and sent all the way back to Arizona to face the music. He had claimed an additional $11,000 selling her possessions.

A web of lies

Upon his arrest, Giovanni claimed his real name was Nikolai Peruskov and that he was born in Siracusa,

Sicily, on April 3rd 1929. His parents, he claimed, had been killed by Nazis when he just eight-years-old. His real name was in fact Fred Jipp, and he was born in New York City on April 3rd 1936.

Because he had specifically used marriage as a means to commit fraud, he was charged with 83 counts of fraud and bigamy. Realising the possible life sentence that may come his way, he offered to plead guilty to bigamy if the fraud charges were dropped.

He then drew up a list of 105 names, his wives who he had technically never divorced. He prepared a chart listing their addresses and dates of marriage, along with an additional list of over 50 names he had used as aliases to fool the system.

After that, he claimed more bizarre tales. He told the court at his trial that he travelled the world and married women he had met at flea markets before becoming scared and running away with the belongings and cash from their bank accounts. He couldn't explain why he did it but didn't think he was hurting anyone.

There was even a claim that he had worked as a contract agent for the CIA in the early 1950s, which is why he became used to using different aliases and secret identities. Some of the names he gave included Frederick Jipp, John Mendoza and John Briccione.

The victims and the fascination

Despite his unusual and damaging behaviour, the courtroom at his trial was packed with women from all walks of life, many of whom had waited outside the courthouse for three hours in order to get a seat inside. During the lunchbreak, they would wait in line so as not to lose the best seats in the house.

When asked why, some of the women claimed it was the best soap opera in town while others were fascinated with Giovanni. Though his large size and criminal behaviour depicted someone unfashionable and gaunt, women were drawn to him.

Sharon Clark was a flea market manager in Indiana who had fallen for Vigliotto shortly before his marriage to Patricia. He had taken her on holiday to Canada and then abandoned her there. He returned to her home and business and disappeared with various antiques and possessions that were later valued at $49,000.

Another victim in New Jersey, 45-year-old Joan Bacarella testified that she was attempting to divorce her previous husband so she could marry Giovanni. But before she could, Giovanni eloped with $40,000 worth of stock from her market business. One of a number of instances where he didn't even marry before committing fraud.

The Pigamist

Many newspapers at the time suggested the term Pigamist as an alternative to bigamist, as there needed to be a new term for someone as prolific as Giovanni.

One of his ruses was to lie to his new wife and claim he had bought a larger house in the next town over. He would then hire a moving van, fill it with their possessions and drive off, stating he would be back to pick them up later. He never did and drove off into the sunset with his haul.

Though we can look at the case of Giovanni and think of it as a fun and bizarre tale of fraud and bigamy, we must never forget the plight of the victims. Playing with someone's love is emotional abuse and is as bad as physical abuse. That Giovanni managed to steal his victim's love as well as they material possessions may have affected them for the rest of their lives.

He used women as a means to get what he wanted, with no motive other than to sleep with new women and take their money to find the next one.

Ultimately, Giovanni – or Fred – was convicted of fraud and bigamy in the case of Patricia and was sentenced to a minimum of 28 years in prison. He died of natural causes in prison in 1991.

'To have married 105 women is greedy and wasteful and suggests a cavalier disregard for natural resources.' – Fred Bruning, Columnist for Maclean's magazine, 1983.

Death of a Seagull

Never before had one bird caused such a flap when a professional baseball player threw a warm-up ball that struck and killed a seagull. What followed next will blow your mind!

When New York Yankees outfielder Dave Winfield, travelled to Toronto to play in a Major League game, he probably didn't expect to accidentally kill a seagull while throwing a ball. He definitely didn't expect to be arrested, charged with animal cruelty, and make Toronto look like a laughing-stock on national television.

More than feathers were flying at the Toronto Exhibition Stadium in Canada, in the middle of that hot Summer in 1983. During the game between the Yankees, and the Toronto Blue Jays, Winfield threw a warm-up ball in the middle of the fifth inning that struck and killed a seagull.

Fans began booing Winfield and some threw rubber balls at him throughout the rest of the game. An official covered the dead seagull with a towel and took it off the field. While the game was still ongoing, it was determined that Winfield should be arrested and charged with the seagull's death.

After the game ended, with a 3-1 win to the Yankees, Winfield was arrested and taken away in handcuffs. Though it had been an accident, the case against him was building, so much so, that the body of the seagull was taken away for a full autopsy to ascertain the cause of death.

You read that right, the seagull was given an autopsy.

Cruelty against animals

Winfield was taken to the Metropolitan Toronto Police 14 Division, where he was charged with causing unnecessary suffering of an animal. Under Canadian law, the offence was punishable by six months in prison or a $500 fine. Toronto manager Pat Gillick paid a $500 bond for Winfield, to release him from custody after one hour at the police station.

As the charge of cruelty against animals was raised to the police, they were obliged to investigate. They connected with the Toronto Humane Society (THS) who assisted them with the autopsy. Michael O'Sullivan, a representative of the THS, suggested they send the body to a nearby University for examination.

That University was the University of Guelph, one of Canada's leading public research facilities. The resident pathologist, Ian Barker, accepted the body of the bird but suggested the cause of death may not be determined despite his very thorough examinations.

Amazingly, Barker checked the bird for all of the following; anaphylaxis, adverse drug reaction, bleed-out, electrocution (lightning), physical trauma (moving vehicle, self-trauma), gunshot, drowning, intestinal accident, botulism, septicaemia (leptospirosis, salmonellosis), heat stroke, poisonous plants (Japanese yew), and other poisons.

Before arriving at the conclusion that the bird was in fact knocked out of the sky by something resembling a baseball.

In addition, he confirmed that the seagull was already sick, had reduced muscle mass, no fat, and would have died within a week if left alone. He found bruises on the brain due to blunt force trauma caused by the baseball hitting the head. Armed with this knowledge, the police had to decide whether to press charges against Winfield.

Feathers were flying

The media jumped on the story and got hold of Winfield as he exited the police station. He told reporters that he turned and whipped the ball to the batboy, but a bird happened to be there. It's unfortunate, he had said, to riotous laughing from the reporters. But he continued and claimed that the fans were on his case about the incident.

Though some residents of Toronto were horrified by the tale of the death of the seagull, others were not quite so concerned. At the time of the seagull's death, Toronto's population of gulls had increased from approximately 10,000 to nearly 200,000 in just a few years. For some residents, Winfield had done them a favour. For others, they thought the charge was absolute rubbish and made them look like idiots.

The National wrote an intro to the story that said Winfield had recorded only three hits during the game; *two baseballs and a seagull*.

After a night of bizarre news reporting and jokes about the dead seagull, the authorities had to decide whether to continue the charges against Winfield. It was down to the Crown attorney to step in and put things right. He said he would make a request to the court to drop the criminal charges because he didn't think Winfield flew afoul of the law.

Invited or extradited

Six months later, long after the charges had been dropped against him, Winfield returned to Toronto to take part in a fundraising event. He spoke to the crowds about the experience of the seagull and his family's reaction to him being invited back to Toronto. Apparently they had said to him; invited or extradited?

Fortunately, Winfield and the local Torontonians saw the funny side of the story, despite showing remorse for the death of the seagull. He had commissioned a painting for the fundraiser that showed a seagull standing in front of a Canadian maple leaf, it went on to sell for $32,000.

So it was with a final twist, that in 1992, Winfield ended up playing for the Toronto Blue Jays as a free agent towards the end of his career. It was the year that the Blue Jays won their first World Series Championship, and the only World Series victory in Winfield's career.

With no seagull deaths in sight.

Vampire of Sacramento

Richard Chase was the poster boy for bizarre serial killers whose tale included Nazi UFOs, necrophilia, cannibalism, drinking blood, and the belief he was turning to powder!

Richard Trenton Chase killed six people over a one month period from 29th December 1977 to 27th January 1978. He became known as the Vampire of Sacramento because he drank the blood of his victims, engaged in necrophilia, and ate some of their remains.

Not the nicest of chaps and we can't make excuses for him but he had a rather bizarre and upsetting childhood. Chase was born in Sacramento in 1950 and was sexually abused by his mother over the first ten years of his life.

He developed a fascination with hurting small animals, like cats and small dogs. It was this feeling of ultimate power over another's life that would eventually drive him to kill a human. He enjoyed torturing and killing small animals, and at the age of 10, Chase killed a cat he found on the street and left its body in the open.

Hurting small animals is one way a child can take out their anger and hatred. They are too small to hurt their abusers and hurt smaller animals until such time when they are big enough to hurt other humans.

During his teen years, he was able to hide his mental issues under a veil of alcohol and marijuana which was easily accessible at the time. He constantly got into trouble at school and at home because of it, but he saw it as an escape from the banalities of life and the troubles that plagued him.

The delusions set in

Chase was unable to perform sexually as he couldn't maintain an erection and this made him feel humiliated and unable to connect with other people. When he was 18, he voluntarily went to see a psychiatrist about his erection problem. It was under the counselling of his psychiatrist where he learned it was sometimes caused by the repression of anger.

After leaving his mother's house on the belief that she was trying to poison him, he rented an apartment with some friends. During his time in the apartment, it was said that Chase enjoyed walking around in the nude and was constantly high on multiple types of drugs including LSD.

Possibly even Orange Sunshine Acid, the story of which is included at the back of this book as a bonus section!

During his time in the apartment he would go through many flatmates, all of which would complain to him and to the authorities about his bizarre behaviour and heavy drug use. One time he nailed the closet door shut in his bedroom because he thought that people were coming out from the darkness and invading his private space.

He began to develop severe paranoia and started to become a fully-fledged hypochondriac, believing that everything was going wrong with his body. At one point, he entered a hospital looking for the person who had stolen his pulmonary artery.

He complained that his bones were coming out through the back of his head causing his skull to split and maintained a belief that his stomach was back to front. He also claimed his heart would stop beating and then start up again after a short amount of time.

Chase would wallow in a pit of paranoid delusions and far-fetched hypochondria, brought on by child abuse and a massive consumption of drugs. When he refused to leave the apartment, his flatmates moved out instead.

His newfound isolation afforded him the possibility of acting on darker desires. He started to trap then kill more small animals. He would disembowel them and eat the raw meat. He then moved onto purchasing small pets with the intention of killing them.

Chase was under the delusion that his heart was shrinking. The consumption of raw flesh and the drinking of animal blood could stop his heart disappearing from his body altogether. He believed this to such an extent that he once injected rabbit blood directly into his veins – which didn't go to well, and he was rushed to hospital, where he got the nickname of Dracula.

Clinical Vampirism

When he was 25-years-old, he was committed as a paranoid schizophrenic to Beverly Manor Institute for the mentally insane. It is reported that anti-psychotic medicines failed to work on him. This could have meant that his schizophrenia and psychosis may have been caused by the drugs that he had previously consumed.

One day, nurses found him with blood around his mouth, they discovered two dead and mutilated birds outside his window that he had lured for capture. It's quite clear that Chase suffered from a mental disorder early on in his life, brought on by physical abuse and humiliation. He may also have been suffering from Renfield Syndrome, a form of clinical Vampirism. After two stints inside the psychiatric hospitals, he was released in late 1976 after being deemed no longer a risk to society. How wrong they were.

He was able to move into another apartment in the city and restarted trapping cats and dogs to kill and consume. In his trial, his mother claimed that Chase appeared on her doorstep one day with a dead cat. He smiled, threw the cat to the ground and ripped it open with his bare hands. Then he smeared the animal's blood all over his neck and face. In an even more bizarre chain of events, his mother failed to contact anyone over the incident.

This was only a few years before he would kill his human victims and drink their blood in a misconstrued belief that he was keeping himself alive. It was because he believed Nazi's had carried out invasive experiments on him causing him to physically need the blood.

Chase was to become synonymous with the term of serial killer. His monstrous crimes are still talked about, discussed, and used as a basis for television shows to this very day. When some people think of serial killers, they might think of schizophrenic individuals who as a child had a tendency for killing small animals and acting bizarrely. Chase fitted every profile available at the time.

From animals to humans

On 29th December 1977, Chase killed Ambrose Griffin, a 51-year-old engineer in the city. After a shopping trip, Griffin returned to his car to get the last of the items. When his wife stepped back outside, she saw her husband on the ground next to the grocery bags. Chase had shot him twice. In hindsight, it was a trial run for darker killings.

One month later, on the evening of 23rd January 1978, Chase attempted to break into a house at 2909 Burnece Street. When a neighbour approached him, he stopped, lit a cigarette, stared at her and casually walked away. That same night, he broke into a house along the street but was interrupted by the owners and he ran off, but not before smearing his excrement on some of their belongings.

He moved down the street to 2360 Tioga Way and casually walked into the home of the Wallin family. He bumped into Teresa Wallin as she was taking out the garbage. Chase shot her three times and dragged her corpse to the bedroom leaving a blood trail through the house. He raped her corpse whilst stabbing her multiple times with a kitchen knife.

Chase then proceeded to carve off her left nipple and cut her torso open below the sternum. He removed her spleen and intestines, cut out her kidneys and sliced her pancreas in half. He then placed the kidneys back inside the body as if they were one organ.

He used a yogurt pot to scoop up the blood from inside her body and drink it. He would then rub her blood over his face and neck. Before he left the house, Chase had gone into the garden, picked up some dog excrement and pushed it into her throat and mouth.

The extreme brutality of the Walling murder was to shock not just California, but the whole of the United States. The media got wind of the story and as the killer seemed to have a fascination with drinking blood, Chase earned the dubious title of 'Vampire of Sacramento'.

Unending blood lust

Four days later, and just one mile from the Wallin house, the Miroth family would suffer a similar, if not worse fate. Chase entered the Miroth residence and shot dead a family friend named Danny Meredith. He stole his wallet and car keys before rampaging through the home.

He shot and killed 38-year-old Evelyn Miroth, her six-year-old son, Jason Miroth, and her 22-month-old nephew, David Ferreira. He raped Evelyn's corpse, cut her open and took some of her organs out before drinking her blood direct from the body. His desire for cannibalism and necrophilia had left nothing to the imagination.

The investigation moved forward very quickly. Chase hadn't tried to hide what he had done. Evidence was easy to come by and when they searched his apartment they found everything they needed to charge, but it wasn't as if they needed to look that hard.

Everything in the kitchen was blood stained, from the fridge to the drinking glasses. One container had pieces of brain fragments and others had small pieces of bone within them. The electric blender had never been cleaned and contained a mixture of blood from numerous animals.

Before his trial, it was claimed Chase virtually turned into an animal when they tried to extract blood from him for a sample. He was subsequently charged with six counts of murder in the first degree, it was a trial that was to last four months during the course of 1978.

On 8th May 1979, after only a few hours, the jury returned the obvious verdict of guilty of six counts of murder in the first degree. He was given the death penalty by gas chamber at San Quentin Prison.

Nazi UFOs and a powdered heart

Chase gave a series of bizarre interviews in which he spoke of his fear of Nazis and UFOs. He believed he had been secretly killed by a combination of both, reanimated, and forced to kill others in order to keep himself alive. He asked the interviewer, FBI Agent Robert Ressler, for a radar gun, so that he could capture the Nazi UFOs and bring them to justice for the murders.

Chase's delusions also led him to believe that his blood was turning to powder and that he needed blood from other creatures to replenish it, as his heart was shrinking. He was to begin an appeal on the basis that he was only killing to preserve his own life.

Needless to say that Chase would go onto become the poster boy for a paranoid schizophrenic serial killer and the type of killer your parents would warn you about before you went to sleep. He was also feared by other prisoners due to the extremely violent nature of his crimes.

On Boxing Day 1980, a guard found him dead in his cell. He had committed suicide with an overdose of antidepressants that he had collected and saved. When Chase's body was autopsied, it was found that his heart was in a perfectly healthy condition.

The Man Who Died Twice

When a fire ripped through a house in Nashville, investigators found the recently deceased body of the owner's husband, which was unusual, as the man had died ten years earlier.

In a bizarre tale of a man who died twice, we look at the mystery behind the two deaths of Clarence Roberts, from Nashville, Indiana.

In 1980, a fire ripped through the small home of Geneva Roberts, razing it to the ground. When investigators searched the burned out residence, they found two bodies, that of Geneva, and also that of Clarence Roberts.

It was an unexpected mystery because Clarence had died in a barn fire on his former property in November 1970, ten years earlier. The body had been identified as Clarence through dental records and personal artefacts and an autopsy showed he had died in the 1980 fire, not the 1970 one.

Except, he was supposed to have died in 1970, because Geneva had tried to get him legally declared dead in 1975. You're going to want to bear with me on this one!

The 1970 fire

And so, investigators had to delve deep into this one, far deeper than they at first suspected. What seemed like a cut and dry accident in rural Nashville was starting to become a bit of a headache.

52-year-old Clarence and his brother, Carson, ran a hardware shop in the city, and were both highly regarded in the community. Clarence had been married to Geneva, his high school sweetheart, for almost thirty years. They raised four children together and acquired luxury cars and eventually the vast property in Nashville.

However, Clarence was living beyond his means, living a champagne lifestyle on a beer budget, and soon he was heavily in debt. Shortly before the 1970 fire, the debt was reaching hundreds of thousands of dollars. His businesses were failing and he was starting to fall behind in bill payments and maintenance on the house.

To cover the debt, Clarence sold the hardware business and invested in property in the area but due to unforeseen maintenance and a downturn in property rentals, the investment collapsed and he was left in more debt than ever before. His other brother, Sheriff Warren Roberts, was forced to repossess the luxury cars and other material items. Clarence and his wife were left in a desperate situation.

One month later, on the same property, one of the barn buildings had caught fire with Clarence Roberts inside. When the flames subsided, investigators pulled the charred body out of the ashes. Though he was burned beyond all recognition, the body was identified as Clarence Roberts.

But there was a mystery afoot at the heart of the Roberts residence.

The mystery homeless man

Two days before the fire, Clarence had been seen talking to an unidentified homeless man near a bar, where he bought dinner for the man and offered him odd jobs around his property. One witness claimed that the homeless man was later laid down on the ground, in front of Clarence, as if Clarence had punched him or knocked him out.

Clarence told some of the patrons of the bar that he was going to take the man to the hospital, except, he never did. The witnesses didn't think anything of it at the time until Clarence was found dead again in 1980.

Despite some reports of suicide by shotgun, others began to suspect that Clarence had faked his own death. It was alleged that Clarence had murdered the homeless man and placed him in the barn, along with his own ring and shotgun, so he could be identified.

It was suggested he did it so that his family could cash in on $1.2million of life insurance policies, to help pay off his debt and have his wife live a better life. Except, she was in on it too!

Clarence's return from the grave

An autopsy of the body in the barn, revealed that the blood type was AB while Clarence had type B. The ring found near the body, which did belong to Clarence, was undamaged by the heat, suggesting it had been thrown in as an afterthought. And just weeks earlier, Clarence had paid for multiple life insurances, to be paid out to his wife upon his death.

By 1975, the insurance companies had refused to pay out, citing lack of irrefutable evidence that the body was indeed Clarence's. There had been no sign of Clarence alive anywhere in the country and his wife tried to have him legally declared dead to help with the insurance but this too was denied by a Nashville court.

Geneva was forced to move to the projects, in a lower-class area, where she lost everything she and her husband had built up over the years. At that point, Clarence was suspected of having murdered the mystery homeless man and faked his death and so a warrant was put out for his arrest.

Between 1975 and 1980, neighbours reported suspicious activity at Geneva's new house. A strange man was often seen lurking around, who made a conscious effort to avoid contacting people. It appeared Clarence had returned to secretly live with his wife.

Clarence had eloped to Mexico after his first death and kept in contact with his wife to ensure the insurance process was moving forward. When the lawsuit against the insurance companies failed in 1975, and he ran out of money, Clarence returned to the States to live with Geneva. Yet, he had to keep it secret because he was meant to be dead.

The theories

In 1980, the second fire burned down Geneva's new home, and two bodies were found, that of Geneva, and her dead husband, Clarence. The first theory was that Clarence had killed Geneva, caused the fire, and tried to fake his death again but was caught in a bizarre accident. At the time of writing, this is the official version of events.

The theory goes that Clarence entered the home, made sure Geneva was passed out and poured flammable liquids over the house. He then set the house alight and went to close the door to the storage room. The room held many solvents and chemicals, and due to the release of smoke from the chemicals, it was suggested that Clarence had passed out and accidentally died in the fire. His body was found in the storage room of the house, surrounded by solvents.

However, though his body was identified for a second time, some people still suspected that he may have faked his death again and that the body belonged to someone else. Another theory pointed to an unidentified killer, who murdered both Clarence and Geneva then set the house alight to cover it up.

Another more sombre theory suggested that the Roberts' killed themselves in the fire, so that their children could get the insurance pay-outs. It's a more likely scenario where two once star-crossed lovers rose to riches, lost everything they had, and saw no other option but to die by their own hand.

A cold case investigation later looked at the man who had died in the 1970 fire and suggested it may have been a drifter from Kentucky but it has never been proven.

Clarence Roberts had died twice, ten years apart, and finally his bizarre story had been put to bed. At least, until the next time he dies.

The Haunting of Fox Hollow Farm

From a violent serial killer to a screaming ghost, the story of Herbie and the haunting of Fox Hollow Farm, is one story that'll send the willies right up you!

American serial killer Herbert Richard Baumeister, AKA: The I-70 Strangler, killed at least 12 young men from 1980 to 1996 and buried their remains at his property on Fox Hollow Farm.

Julie Baumeister believed her new husband, Herbie, to be a good-natured local businessman who had done well for himself – despite the medical skeletons in the garage.

She had married him in 1971 and they had three children together which bolstered their relationship. Her 24-year-old husband was nothing if not a hard worker, and a real catch at a time when he was becoming involved in expanding his business and growing his mini-empire.

By 1988, Herb had founded and opened the Sav-A-Lot chain of stores in Indiana. This helped strengthen his position with business leaders in the area, and he became a respected member of the local community.

Except, Herb was already hiding a deep, dark secret, that involved the rape and murder of young men. He was able to hide his true evil from the world around him, including Julie and their children. Yet, his path to darkness had begun many years before meeting the love of his life.

Dead crows and schizophrenia

Born in 1947, shortly after World War Two had ended, Herbie was raised in a relatively normal household with three younger siblings. But when he reached puberty, something had already changed within him.

He became antisocial and withdrew from his friends and family, cutting himself off from the world around him. Something had snapped inside of him and it seemed there had been no obvious catalyst for it. Some of his friends at school later claimed he played with the bodies of dead animals and was once caught urinating on a teacher's desk.

A former friend believed something wasn't right with Herb and recalled a story about a dead crow. One morning on the way to school, Herb had picked up a dead crow and stuffed it into his pocket. He rubbed the feathers and blood on his trouser legs. When he got to school, he yanked the crow out of his pocket, and slammed it on the teacher's desk, in full view of the class.

Horrified, the teacher removed him from the room, and ordered he be sent to a psychiatrist. While a teenager, Herb was diagnosed by a doctor as having schizoaffective disorder, but due to the difference in mental health access we have nowadays compared to then, he was not given any psychiatric treatment for it. His mind was allowed to fester in his own loneliness, conjuring up all manner of horrific ideas.

Skeletons and manipulation

By 1991, three years after creating a successful business, Herb moved his family into a large Tudor-style home and estate in the fashionable Westfield district of Indiana. The property had a swimming pool, stables, and almost 20 acres of land where the family could grow and live in luxury.

The property was called Fox Hollow Farm, a former working farm that had been converted into a liveable residence many years earlier. The success of his businesses meant that Herb could afford to purchase the residence.

Inside the house, however, a tension and a fear was rising. Unbeknownst to Julie, Herb was able to control her with his manipulative personality and controlling ways. She began to believe everything her husband was telling her, including that the mysterious freshly dug holes around the farm were for irrigation purposes.

Julie split from Herb multiple times but always returned to him, in a fashion that some would describe as Herb having control over his wife. When colleagues and friends visited the house, they saw messy rooms, unclean surfaces and a complete lack of order.

The grounds of the property had been left to overgrow and their land was becoming unusable. Exactly the type of grounds that Herb needed to hide the growing number of bodies he was burying on the farm.

At around the same time, one of the Baumeister's children was playing in the grounds when they unearthed a complete human skeleton. Julie and the children were in shock and they waited for Herb to return to find out what was going on. When he arrived home, he dismissed the discovery and explained it away as being one of his father's fake medical skeletons he'd had in storage for some time.

Herb claimed to have found it in the garage one day and decided to bury it with no explanation as to why.

Julie believed her husband was telling the truth but the truth was far more shocking. The skeleton belonged to one of his victims.

Missing gay men

In 1993, connections in the cases of missing gay men from the area were already being put together by a private investigator named Vergil Vandagriff. He joined forces with an investigator from the Indianapolis Police Department, named Mary Wilson. Together, they threw themselves into the cases of the missing men, believing they may have been connected in some way.

They worked on the investigation to connect the evidence they had in front of them. As the case gained media attention and the names of the missing were made public, they were approached by a mystery gay man who claimed he knew who killed a friend of his. He gave them a name but the name didn't show up on any searches and so it was filed as another statement.

The mystery man disappeared for a couple of years until 1995 when he phoned the investigation and gave them the number plate of the man who he suspected to have killed his friend. It has long remained unclear whether he had carried out his own private investigation in order to get the license plate, or whether he had been holding onto it until the right time came around.

The license plate linked to Herb Baumeister, and so Wilson approached Fox Hollow Farm to speak to him. She asked to search the house but he refused immediately and slammed the door in her face. When Wilson returned with police, Julie refused them entry. As the only link was a license plate, the investigation couldn't gain a warrant for the house.

Unearthing the bodies

Behind the scenes, the marriage was falling apart and Julie was becoming scared of her husband. His violent mood swings and weird behaviour had become too much for her to handle. He would sometimes stand outside for hours simply staring into the woods. By June 1996, Julie had finally ended her marriage to Herb, yet they still lived at the farm together.

Suspecting that her former husband had been up to no good, she waited for him to leave on his next business trip, and then called the police. Julie brought in the investigators and allowed them to search the house and the grounds without a warrant.

Within 48 hours, the remains of 11 men were unearthed, with only four of them ever being identified. It remains unclear how Herb found out about the search of the house, but he did. Before a warrant went out for his arrest, he eloped over the Canadian border to Ontario.

He wrote a suicide note in which he spoke about his failing marriage and dwindling business but didn't mention the murders at all. Some believed it was the last control he had left. Shortly after, he shot himself dead in Pinery Provincial Park.

Julie went on to tell the investigation that Herb had made over 100 journeys to Ohio on apparent business trips. It was then that the investigation linked him with the murders of nine more men, whose bodies had been discovered along the main highway between Indiana and Ohio; the Interstate 70, which gave him the moniker of the I-70 Strangler

Herb's body was discovered eight days after he had killed himself.

The Fox Hollow Farm hauntings

After the investigation had come to an end, Fox Hollow Farm and its buildings were stripped of everything. The grounds were left to overgrow and the property stood abandoned for many years, a grim reminder of the bodies buried there.

That was until it was sold cheaply to Rob and Vicky Graves from Indiana, who jumped on the low price and began rebuilding the farm and buildings. It was a dream home, ripe for refurbishment and a new couple to grow into.

Everything seemed to be going fine until one day Vicky was cleaning the house and the hoover kept coming unplugged at the wall socket for no apparent reason. It scared her and she began to suspect something was wrong with the house but couldn't put a finger on it. The same day, she started hoovering another room but it stopped working. She looked back to the wall socket, and yet again, the plug had come away from the wall.

But that was only the beginning.

One day, Vicky came home from work to see Rob painting a wonderful piece of art. She stood behind him and had a good look at his work. Suddenly, she noticed a man outside of the window, a few metres away standing in the grounds of the house.

The man turned from the window and moved away but he had no legs. Shocked, Vicky stumbled back, watching with horror as the ghostly man disappeared completely. Directly after that incident, the Graves' installed security cameras but nothing happened for weeks.

The screaming ghost of one of Herb's victims

Shortly after, one of Rob's work colleagues named Joe, moved into the spare apartment in the property, with his dog. He was helping out with the grounds and paying a small amount of rent to help them with the finances.

One night while washing the dishes, there was a knock at the door. Joe opened it but no one was there. He walked outside and felt a strange chill in the air but couldn't see anyone on the property. Then his dog began acting as if someone was in the room behind him, but upon closer inspection, they were alone in the apartment.

Joe put it down to tiredness – until a few nights later. He was walking his dog in the grounds when he saw a shadowy man watching them from the treeline. The dog gave chase and Joe followed, to try and get a closer look but the man disappeared. He ran back to the house and locked the door. The same night, he spoke to Vicky about his experiences, and it appeared they had seen the same ghostly man.

Another night came and another encounter happened. This time, the dog was growling at someone who was attempting to open the front door. The handle was shaking up and down and the door pushing against its hinges. As Joe neared the door, it suddenly swung open and a gust of wind blew into the apartment.

He traipsed to the door and looked outside but no one was there. Except, he could hear someone breathing nearby. Upon turning to head back through the door, he saw a bloodied man running towards him from inside the apartment, screaming for his life. Joe screamed back and covered his face. When he removed his arms, the man had vanished, and only the gust of wind remained.

Joe and the Graves' then began to research Baumeister's victims. As they watched some old news footage, Joe was certain that one of the victims on the list was the man he had seen running towards him.

On yet another occasion, Joe's dog uncovered a human bone in the grounds of the estate, in the exact location he had first seen the man in the woods. It seemed that the victims of Herb Baumeister were reaching out from beyond the grave.

Paranormal investigators and demonologists descend on the farm

Rob Graves then contacted Mary Wilson, the lead investigator on the case. She came out to the estate and showed them where the bodies had been uncovered. They appeared to be in the same vicinity as the locations of the unexplained phenomena.

News of the hauntings grew and an army of paranormal investigators and demonologists descended on the estate to record any instances of supernatural activity. Though there weren't allowed to stay in the Graves' home, Joe was able to borrow some of the equipment from them.

On one occasion, Joe was in the pool with some others, cleaning the bottom of it, when cold fingers grabbed his neck and pulled him under the water. He escaped and charged out of the pool, screaming at the others to get out before the demon attacked them. The others who were with him claimed the water had become ice cold shortly before Joe was attacked.

Another night brought another haunting. Joe was at the computer working when he heard a knife scratching against the wall, he went to look and found a knife on the floor. Using the new experience he had gained from the paranormal investigators, he unplugged all the electrics and used his phone to record any unheard noises.

Afterwards, he replayed the recording and a voice crackled through the audio.

"I am the married one."

Because all his victims had been gay men, it was believed to be the voice of Herb Baumeister. It appeared he had returned to Fox Hollow Farm to haunt those who ventured there. The Graves' moved out of the property soon after and never returned.

Instead, week in and week out, there are paranormal investigators on site, believing the property and grounds to be amongst the most haunted in Indiana. On one occasion, a large team of investigators arrived at the estate and stayed for six months. The team included a physics expert, a demonologist, EVP and visual specialist, and an army of psychics.

It appeared to them, at least, that evil never dies.

The Disappearance of Bobby Dunbar

A missing boy is returned to his parents eight months after disappearing. Finally, the family can move on, except, the boy that had come back was not their son at all.

Over 100 years ago, in 1912, on a hot Summer's night in the Bayou, Louisiana, the Dunbar family were weekend-tripping out near a lake when the unthinkable happened, their eldest son went missing.

Lessie and Percy Dunbar were fishing the crocodile-infested Swayze Lake in St. Landry Parish, Louisiana, with their four-year-old son Robert 'Bobby' Clarence and two-year-old son Alonzo. The moon was high in the sky and the water was smooth and steady but the fish had not been forthcoming.

At some point during the night, when Lessie and Percy were sleeping, Bobby had crawled out of his tent and vanished without a trace. They searched the location they were in and walked the lake to see where he had gone to but there was no sign of him. Immediately they raised the alarm and called the police.

But what began as a missing persons story was soon to become far more bizarre.

Eight months later

The story of the missing boy was so well known at the time that newspapers from across the country were running the story. It was to be with some fortune that the beginning of the tale ended with some good luck.

After eight months of investigations and searching for Bobby, the Dunbar's had good news. An investigation had found their son, 200 miles away in Mississippi. It appeared he had been abducted by a piano tuner named William Cantwell Walters, from North Carolina.

He had been travelling with a boy who had matched Bobby's description.

William was shocked at the accusation and claimed the boy was Charles Bruce Anderson, son of Julia Anderson, and that he had been granted custody to look after him for a couple of days. Despite the story, the Dunbar's were transported to Mississippi to be reunited with their son. Investigators were adamant the boy was the missing Bobby Dunbar.

During what can only be described as a terribly emotional scene, the boy who investigators believed was Bobby Dunbar, was snatched away from William, and taken into temporary care to be identified by the Dunbar's. And identify him, they did, in fact the Dunbar's were certain they had found their missing son.

Except, they hadn't.

Muddying the waters

Newspaper reports from the time were as muddled as they are today, with the same level of bias and misinformation we have come to expect from the industry. One account claimed the boy had immediately run towards Lessie, shouting 'mother' at the top of his voice, then embraced her with both of them crying together.

Another claimed that Lessie seemed uncertain as to what was going on and simply watched in horror as the boy cried to himself, unsure of where to turn. The same report stated that Lessie was unsure if the boy was indeed Bobby. Immediately – questions!

We're not talking a lost pet here, we're talking about a missing boy, a real-life human. Imagine if your child had gone missing for half a year. Would you still recognise them after eight months? Would you still feel that parental connection to them? Would you run into each other's arms? Yes, to all three, I would imagine, and hope.

To have such wildly different newspaper reports of the same event has to make us wonder if the reporters were even at the scene. Why did one state Lessie was unsure and the other claim the boy called her mother? The truth is, they probably all thought they were correct. There would have been crying, confusion, and misunderstanding at the reunion.

It was rare after all, that such a young missing child would ever be returned to their parents after eight months of disappearance. Some reporters would have been so caught up in the fanfare of the reunion that their own emotions would have run wild.

The Dunbar's returned to their hometown of Opelousas, Louisiana, and were welcomed home by the locals and local press. The local press again had varying reports of how the boy interacted with the Dunbar's younger son, Alonzo. One claimed that the boy recognised Alonzo immediately, and the other claimed that the boy had no recognition of him at all.

Still, all was settled a few days later, after Lessie confirmed to the press that the missing boy was indeed her son, Bobby. She had bathed him the day after they returned home and was able to identify the boy's moles and scars.

Julia Anderson

The transfer of the boy to the Dunbar's happened so fast, with such confidence, that Julia Anderson, the supposed mother of the boy, had no time to intervene. Anderson worked as a handyperson for the Walters family and was unmarried, which was frankly frowned upon in those days.

She told authorities that the boy they had taken to the Dunbar's was not Bobby, but was in fact, her son, Charles. She had allowed Walters to take her son on his trip to visit relatives as the family were close to her and her son.

Due to her work with the Walters, and the fact she was unmarried, Julia was unable to afford to take the Dunbar's to court and reclaim her son. But investigators gave her the benefit of the doubt and organised a line-up with five different boys, including the one who she claimed was her son and had been returned to the Dunbar's.

Again, we have this through newspaper reports, but when the returned boy was paraded in front of her, she was unable to identify him, and the boy didn't seem to show any recognition of her. The newspapers ran with that version of events and even dragged Julia's name through the mud, claiming she was an undesirable out to cause pain to a well-off family who had already suffered.

Still, the patient investigators gave her one more chance to prove the boy was her son. She was allowed to strip him and point out various marks on his body that proved he belonged to her. Except, she said at the time she had a strong certainty the boy was hers. Realistically, one would know if a child was theirs or not, and the uncertainty from both sides was beginning to catch on.

Julia's claims were ultimately dismissed and she was later brought to the trial of Walters, who had been charged with abducting Bobby Dunbar. Around the same time, the residents of the town of Poplarville, where Walters lived, were beginning to rally around him and Julia.

The residents of the community were familiar with Walters and Julia's son, and claimed they had seen them together, long before Bobby Dunbar had disappeared. Some of them even took to the stand in the abduction case to testify that the boy was not Bobby Dunbar but was Julia's son.

Despite all of the evidence that the boy was Charles Bruce Anderson, the court and judge convicted Walters of kidnapping Bobby Dunbar, and sentenced him to life in prison. The boy that everyone claimed was Charles, was raised as Bobby Dunbar with the Dunbar family.

The passage of time

Julia became well known in Poplarville and went on to become a devout Christian, marrying a local man, and raising seven children. The community rallied around her and looked after her with the steadfast belief that the Dunbar's had orchestrated the kidnapping of her son to replace their own.

Two years after being in prison, Walters won an appeal and was given a new trial. However, due to the massive costs of the first trial, the courts declined to try him again and he was ultimately released. Until the end of his life in 1945, he would constantly proclaim his innocence with the belief that the boy was indeed Julia's son.

Bobby Dunbar was raised by the Dunbar family as their own. He went on to marry and have four children of his own. He died in 1966 and was buried in the Dunbar's hometown. And then, the truth, at least part of it, was revealed.

In 2004, 92 years after Bobby Dunbar first disappeared, renewed interest in the case prompted DNA testing to resolve the case once and for all. Bob Dunbar Jr., who was Bobby Dunbar's son, agreed to be tested. The results showed that Dunbar Jr. was not related by blood to Alonzo Dunbar, the younger brother of Bobby Dunbar. DNA testing also showed that the boy had genetic relations to the Anderson bloodline. This meant, that after 92 years, Julia Anderson and Walters had been vindicated. The boy raised as Bobby Dunbar was indeed Charles Bruce Anderson, her son.

So what happened to Bobby Dunbar?

In 2008, one of Julia Anderson's sons, named Hollis, told a reporter that back in the Forties, Bobby Dunbar, or Charles Anderson, as we know now, visited him at his place of business. And he wasn't the only one to recount a similar story.

Another of Julia's children claimed that Charles had come to visit her also and they spoke at great length about the area, the community, and the story of Bobby Dunbar. It seemed that Charles himself was unsure whether he was the Dunbar's son.

Today, many of Charles Anderson's grandchildren continue to live as Dunbar's, as that was how they were raised. But in a heart-warming meet and greet around the same time, the Dunbar's met with the Anderson grandchildren and both sides were welcomed.

So, if Charles Anderson was raised as Bobby Dunbar then what happened to the real Bobby Dunbar? The truth is we may never know but one theory suggests that Bobby fell into the lake and drowned or was eaten by a crocodile, which were common in Louisiana lakes – or swamps.

Another grimmer theory is that he was abducted from the side of the lake by an unidentified person or persons. From there, he would either have been killed, or more shockingly, raised within another but this time unsuspecting family. However, the crocodile theory seemed more likely.

If the Dunbar's were unsure whether the boy was their son, then why did they accept him? Perhaps they did believe the boy was Bobby, and whether they were lying to themselves or not, they raised him as their own.

Perhaps we'll never know the reasons why they claimed a boy that wasn't their own. Not many of us will lose a child in our lifetimes and we will always struggle to understand what it must feel like and the intense emotion related to it.

What is certain is that the real Bobby Dunbar vanished on a hot Summer's day in Louisiana in 1912 and was never found again.

"Dear sir, in view of human justice to Julia Anderson and mothers, I am prompted to write to you. I sincerely believe the Dunbar's have Bruce Anderson and not their boy. If this is their child, why are they afraid for anyone to see or interview him privately?" – a letter to the Walters lawyer from a Christian woman of Poplarville, dated 1913.

The Matrix Defence

A killer who brutally murdered his landlady was found not guilty as he had been sucked into the Matrix and was living in a computer-generated dream world. Yeah, this happened – twice!

There have been many bizarre reasons in killer's defence trials over the years, but perhaps no more so than the Matrix Defence, based solely on the belief that the killer was living in a dream-simulation.

You've heard of the movie, The Matrix, but the film managed to infiltrate places you might not have realised. The late Nineties sci-fi film explores the possibility that reality as we believe it to be, is in fact a computer-generated dream world, created by machines in the future, to keep the human race docile.

A great premise for a sci-fi film that ended up becoming a legitimate defence in court cases across America. It became known as the Matrix Defence. It would have been unusual but acceptable for it to have been used once. Yet, it was used twice – successfully.

No consequences

In San Francisco, in the year 2000, after having viewed the film on multiple occasions, 27-year-old University student, Vadim Mieseges, killed his landlady. For no other reason than he believed he was living in the Matrix and his consequences didn't matter.

The clean-cut Swiss-born computer science student was renting a room in an apartment owned by 47-year-old landlady and Laguna Honda Hospital administrator Ella Wong. The apartment block in the well-to-do Richmond District was close to the University and he had been renting it since the beginning of the year.

Ella, a Hong Kong native, was a warm, quiet woman who was mostly dedicated to her work. She helped out in the community and was generally well-regarded. To cover her finances, she took in Vadim as a lodger after he answered an advertisement for the spare room. She would have had no idea, that Vadim would be drawn into the film so much that he would go on to kill her.

Ella's neighbour, Dee Chiu, was the last person to see her alive. She had last seen her as she left to go to church on a cool Spring Sunday. Dee also claimed that she got on well with Vadim and that he was an upstanding gentleman who seemed to have no bad bone in him and certainly didn't look like a killer. How wrong she was.

On the Monday, when Ella failed to show for work, her colleagues and family raised the alarm and reported her missing. Her car was found outside of her apartment with her diabetes insulin inside which meant that Ella must have still been inside the apartment.

When police entered the property, there was no sign of her but the phone had been ripped from the wall, The bed was made, and everything else seemed to have its place. It seemed that Ella had walked off somewhere without letting her work know. Except, one thing was missing; the lodger.

Skinned and dismembered

A couple of hours later, after police put out a warrant for Vadim's arrest, they discovered his car a few blocks from the residence. It had been abandoned and vandalised and there were signs of a struggle inside. The investigations learned that he had not turned up to the University on the Monday morning.

On the Monday afternoon, officers got a call from a Macy's store at the Stonestown shopping mall. A man matching Vadim's description had vandalised the mannequins and broken them open. He had removed a wooden rod from one of them, pretended it was a sword, and was attacking people. The guards struggled to overpower him and called the police in to help.

It took two officers and two security guards to finally overpower Vadim and wrestle him to the ground, despite him biting them wherever he could. The officers found him to be disorientated and confused, claiming he had gone to the store to steal the TV sets that had once belonged to him – they hadn't.

While he was being arrested, they removed a knife from him, along with various drugs. He suddenly blurted out that he had killed Ella and cut her body into little pieces but gave no reason why. Later that night, he led police to a garbage bin in Golden Gate Park, where they were met with a horrific sight.

In a bag, pushed into the bin, was the upper torso of Ella. She had been stabbed to death and chopped up, just as Vadim had said. Not only that, but he had also skinned and disembowelled her, then cut her up and scattered her body parts across the city in various garbage bins.

They found body parts in two other bins and spent the next week searching for the rest. They never found all of Ella's body parts, suspecting some had been dumped into the water.

Warped perception of reality

At first, police suspected the murder had come about due to a rent dispute or that Ella had stumbled across Vadim doing drugs in his room. The truth was far more bizarre.

Back home in Switzerland, a year before he moved to the United States to study, Vadim had been sent to a psychiatric hospital for a personality disorder. He was institutionalised a second time shortly before leaving the country.

Before the case went to trial, his defence lawyers had prepared a rather unusual defence strategy. According to Vadim, he believed that he was living in the Matrix and claimed that Ella was emitting evil vibes through a digital aura surrounding her body. Fearing being stuck in the Matrix forever, the only *sane* thing to do was to kill her and cut up the body.

Vadim's psychiatric issues had got the better of him and his paranoia, combined with excessive crystal meth use, had warped his perception of reality. It was suspected that had police not caught him when they did, then he may have skinned and dismembered more people.

The judge accepted the bizarre insanity plea and the case never went to trial. Vadim was found incompetent to stand trial and was sectioned in a psychiatric institute indefinitely. Regardless of whether he really believed he was in the Matrix or not, the defence had worked. And ultimately, the Matrix defence was used again – and again.

Two years later, in July 2002, 36-year-old bartender Tonda Lynn Ansley killed her own landlady. Sherry Lee Corbett was walking along a street in Hamilton, Ohio, when Tonda shot her three times with a handgun. During interviews after her arrest, Tonda claimed that Corbett and three other potential victims, including her own husband, had been controlling her mind.

She claimed they would enter her dreams in the night while she slept and make her have dreams she neither wanted nor could cope with. She believed she was being drugged in her sleep, taken away into the real world, then replaced each night with a new body, to awake in the world that had been designed by the people around her. Again, a judge accepted her Matrix Defence and the case never went to trial.

One year later, in Virginia, 19-year-old Joshua Cooke murdered his adoptive parents with a shotgun. He had been lying in bed, listening to heavy metal music, when he looked over at a poster of the Matrix and realised he was living within it. He grabbed his shotgun and marched downstairs to commit murder.

The Matrix Defence was put forward to the judge at his pre-trial and the judge was about to accept the plea when Cooke pleaded guilty. He was sentenced to 40 years for murder but still claimed to be living in the Matrix.

In the early 2000's at least, it appeared that claiming real life was a simulation, was one defence to get away with murder.

The Shark Arm Murder Case

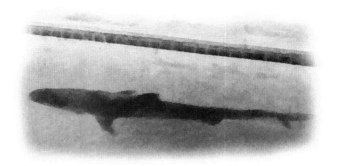

In Sydney, a captive tiger shark vomited a human arm, sparking an investigation that led to one of the most bizarre murder cases you'll ever read.

In Sydney, Australia, in the warm Spring of the Great Depression of 1935, aquarium owner Bert Hobson was looking for a new attraction for his business, the Coogee Aquarium and Swimming Baths. What better attraction in the 1930s than a real-life shark!

To entice customers back to the park, Bert and his son went fishing off the coast of Coogee in the hopes of a big enough catch to wow the crowds. Sure enough, they caught a 14-foot tiger shark, weighing over one-ton. Somehow, they managed to transport the shark back to one of their pools and a new attraction was born.

The Aquarium reopened for the season ahead and the crowds flooded in. For one group of spectators on that Spring day, way back when, it was a day they would never forget.

Shark vomit!

To coincide with Anzac Day, a national day of remembrance in Australia and New Zealand, the shark became the special attraction. Hundreds of families with children descended on the Coogee Aquarium and gathered around to see the tiger shark in its open tank.

Suddenly, and without warning, the shark vomited the left hand and forearm of a human man. The arm floated in the tank for an hour, in front of all the day trippers and families before Bert managed to fish it out. Alongside the arm were the remains of a rat and bird.

The arm had not been digested and had recognisable tattoos all over it. Bert immediately called in the police to see if they knew of any accidents nearby or missing people. They didn't and so there was only one thing to do – kill the shark.

After the shark had been cut open they found the remains of a smaller shark inside. A forensic specialist looked at what they had found and deduced that the man, or at least part of him had been eaten by the smaller shark which was then eaten by the tiger shark. No other remains of the man were found.

Using new fingerprint technology and the tattoo of two boxers still visible on the arm, they were able to identify the arm's original owner. His name was Jimmy Smith, a 45-year-old Englishman born in England in 1890. He had emigrated to Australia after a failed boxing career and became a small-time criminal and local boatman. He was reported missing just a couple of weeks earlier.

Almost immediately, the investigation turned to that of a solved missing person case, to that of a homicide. The arm had the remnants of a rope attached to the wrist and it was clear it had been cut off rather than chewed. The shark attack victim quickly turned into a murder victim.

Murder

They discovered that Jimmy worked for a Sydney-based smuggler who had helped fund his boating business, and from there the plot thickened. The smuggler turned businessman was named Reginald

William Lloyd Holmes. He ran a large boat building business at Lavender bay in New South Wales and had paid cash to Jimmy on the side to work on insurance scams for him. There had been a case in 1934 where a pleasure cruiser named Pathfinder was sunk. Pathfinder had been over-insured and Holmes' business received the pay-outs.

He was also suspected of using speedboats to run cocaine drops from passing ships along the Sydney shoreline. Realising he had found a criminal confidant in Jimmy, Holmes forged ahead with a partnership with Patrick Francis Brady, an ex-serviceman and convicted forger.

The plan was to use signatures obtained from Holmes' business clients, to forge cheques and cash them in at various locations around Australia. Jimmy, ever the criminal entrepreneur, realised he could make more money on the side by secretly blackmailing Holmes. Holmes had found out and decided the best way to deal with the problem was to have him killed.

Jimmy was last seen drinking at the Cecil Hotel and playing cards with Brady. The next day, Jimmy was reported missing by his unsuspecting wife, believing he had gone on a fishing trip with friends. Turns out that in some bizarre way, Jimmy did go fishing.

Shark food and a botched suicide

Port Hacking and Gunnamatta Bay were searched by the Australian Navy and the Air Force, but the rest of Jimmy's body was never found. On the night of the murder, Brady had waited for Jimmy to return home then – being the master murderer he was – booked a taxi from Cecil Hotel to take him to, you guessed it, Holme's house. When the media got hold of the story of the murdered man in the belly of the shark, the taxi driver contacted police and identified Brady to them.

He said that Brady was disorientated and dishevelled and clearly hiding something under his jacket. Brady had lured Jimmy out of his home to a cottage that he had rented for the night. It was suspected he shot Jimmy in the head before dismembering his body. He was then alleged to have taken a boat from Holmes' yard and dispersed Jimmy's body into the ocean.

Brady was arrested for the murder and the evidence against him was overwhelming. Except, the prosecution had one major problem, there was no body. In 1930s Australia, and indeed in many countries across the world, if there was no body then there was no proof that a murder ever took place, despite having one body part, such as an arm.

Four days after Brady had been arrested, Holmes was seen walking into his boatshed with a gun. He shot himself in the head. Which normally would have killed someone – but this is bizarre true crime! The bullet that exited the gun flattened against his forehead instead of passing through, knocking him out.

Holmes fell into the water where he was instantly brought back to consciousness. While witnesses were calling the police, Holmes managed to climb into one of his speedboats and speed off. He led police boats and the coastguard on a bizarre two hour chase around Sydney Harbour before he was finally knocked off the boat and captured – and taken to hospital.

The murders continue

After he was released from hospital, Holmes agreed to help police with their investigation and claimed that it was indeed Brady who had killed Jimmy but he himself was in no way involved. He said Brady had come to his home the evening of the murder, brandishing Jimmy's arm and blackmailed him for £500 Australian pounds (the currency of Australia from 1910 to 1966). Holmes paid the blackmail.

On June 11th, many weeks after the investigation had begun, Holmes was found dead in his car at Dawes Point, shot three times execution style. The execution was made to look as though it had been a suicide but the police saw right through the façade.

Holmes had been due to testify at Brady's trial the same day and his death meant the inquest had lost their star witness. The conclusion of the inquest was that an arm did not mean the owner of the arm was dead and that Jimmy could have still been alive somewhere. The case was thrown out of court and Brady was acquitted.

Later theories suggested that Jimmy may have been assassinated on the orders of gangland boss Eddie Weyman, who had been arrested a year earlier supposedly on information that Jimmy had provided to police. It was also theorised that Holmes took a contract out on his own life, in order for his family to get the life insurance and avoid the embarrassment of trial.

Of course, we wouldn't have known any of this if Bert Hobson and his son hadn't decided they needed a shark for their aquarium. A shark that spat out a human arm.

Mystery of the Body in the Tree

In 1940s England, a group of young boys were playing in the forest when they found a dead woman stuffed into the middle of a wych elm tree.

Hagley Wood on first sight is a beautiful English forest in Worcestershire, but it holds a macabre secret that has never been solved. In April 1943, while World War Two was still going on, four local boys, Robert Hart, Thomas Willetts, Bob Farmer and Fred Payne, ventured onto the private land of Lord Cobham, known as Hagley Estate.

They were out searching for birds' nests to steal their eggs, an old English pastime for kids with nothing else to do. While searching for the perfect location to begin their hunt, they ventured to Wychbury Hill and found themselves staring at a large dead wych elm tree. Believing it to be a perfect location for nesting birds, Farmer began climbing.

Pushed on by his friends, he got to the top of the trunk and looked down into the middle of the tree. There, at the bottom of the tree was a skull, which wasn't uncommon for forests in England, due to the proliferation of wildlife. However, the skull had hair. Curious, he reached down and lifted the skull out of the tree to show his friends.

On realising the skull had human teeth, they found the rest of the skeleton inside the tree. Suddenly they realised they were on private land and threw the skull back into the tree and ran away from the location. The boys returned home and decided not to tell anyone about what they had found. Except, Farmer felt uneasy about what he had found and eventually told his parents.

Investigation

The next morning, police descended onto Wychbury Hill and began their investigation. They found the near-complete skeletal remains of a female, along with various items of clothing and a gold wedding ring. When the area was searched, the bones of her missing hand were found a short distance away.

Forensic testing showed that the female had been dead for at least eighteen months and was suspected to have been suffocated to death, due to remnants of a cloth found in her mouth. The body would have been placed inside the tree at the time of her death, while it was still warm. Had it been subjected to rigor mortis then the body would not have fitted inside.

Due to the upheaval of the war, identification of the body became difficult. Too many people were being reported missing on a weekly, if not daily basis, for the police to cross reference each and every one of them. The investigation ground to a halt. Despite her dentistry being unique, there was no match forthcoming and her case went cold almost immediately.

Until the graffiti began.

Meme before memes

One year after the discovery of the body and failure of the investigation, mysterious graffiti began appearing around the local area and then the whole of the country. The first of the graffiti was spotted in Birmingham, twelve miles away from Hagley Wood.

It read; *Who Put Bella In The Wych Elm*.

For some bizarre reason, the graffiti took hold and multiplied across the country, becoming synonymous with the body in the tree. It was clear that despite the case running cold, someone had not forgotten what happened to the person they called Bella.

The Bella graffiti continued appearing on walls, gravestones, and trees, and has never stopped appearing. Bella had become more famous in death than in life but still, her real identity had never been solved, and her suspect remained uncaptured.

Close to the summit of Wychbury Hill, just 150 metres from the West Midlands border, is a monument known as the Wychbury Obelisk, or Hagley Obelisk, visible for miles around. Every Spring, the same graffiti, written to be in the same handwriting style appears on the monument.

The theories

The name of Bella first appeared with the graffiti and had not been proposed by anyone before that. Had the killer created the first of the graffiti? Did someone know who the victim was and never came forward to identify her? These questions and more have haunted cold case investigators for years and have led to various theories about her death and her identity.

In 1941, a German spy named Josef Jakobs parachuted into England but injured himself on landing and was captured shortly after. He claimed that his lover, whom he had a photo of, had also just landed in England, after being trained as a spy, but no trace of her entering the country ever existed. In 2016, it was concluded that his lover, Clara Bauerle, had died in a German hospital around the same time.

In a 1944 Birmingham police report, a Brummie sex worker reported that another prostitute named Bella, which was short for Luebella, had disappeared at about the time the body in the tree was said to have been killed. The case was never followed up by police and the report is the only record of the missing prostitute named Bella.

In 1945, a London archaeologist, Margaret Murray, claimed that the death was a result of witchcraft. The hand that had been found away from the body had been cut off as part of a ritual. She believed the murder had been carried out by occult gypsies during a ritual called the Hand of Glory. The press at the time seemed to favour the story of witchcraft and ran with it for many years.

Many more theories emerged over the years, including one that the victim was a Dutch national who had been killed by a German spy-ring. Another that Lord Cobham had her killed at an occult party on his estate. And yet another bizarre theory that Bella hadn't been found dead but that she was growing inside of the tree, due to the hair on the skull.

What happened to Bella?

One of the most logical, yet more disregarded theories comes from Hagley itself, but ten years after the incident.

In 1953, a police report shows that local Hagley resident, Una Mossop, went to the police after her ex-husband, Jack Mossop, had confessed to the murder before the body was even found. Jack and a Dutchman named Van Ralt, had been out drinking one night when they met a woman in the Lyttelton Arms in Hagley. The three of them got drunk together and left the pub later in the evening.

As they were driving through the village, the woman had passed out. Unsure what to do, they took her to a hollow tree in the woods, placed her inside, and assumed she had woken up in the morning and gone home. He confessed to his family the week after but they didn't believe it, instead finding him to be crazy.

Jack was confined to a psychiatric institute shortly after. He claimed to have nightmares of a girl staring at him from within the forest and that the forest was alive. Unfortunately, he died long before the body was even found by Farmer and his friends.

It has long remained unclear why Una waited a decade to retell his story, or why she had kept it secret for so long. There are no psychiatric records available to ascertain whether Jack was indeed having nightmares of the girl in the forest. If he had, then his story could have been a version of the truth.

It may also stand to reason that the woman getting drunk in the pub with them, was a prostitute named Luebella who had been reported missing. Despite the story, it has long been debunked by those who favour tales of witchcraft.

We may never know what happened to Bella or who she really is but her story continues to persist to this day. In England, in 2018, there was a 75th anniversary event of Bella's discovery, three miles away from the elm tree. It included authors, filmmakers, paranormal investigators, and live Bella-themed music!

Curiously, Bella's skeleton and original autopsy report are missing and have never been found, only adding to the mystery of the body in the tree.

Factory of Death

When a Russian maniac built an underground textiles factory, he began recruiting females, not as workers but to fulfil his twisted dream of owning an army of slaves.

Alexander Komin, AKA: The Vyatka Maniac or Vyatskiye Maniac, was a Russian serial killer and criminal who killed at least four people over a two year period in the mid-1990s. The case became known as one of Russia's most disturbing crimes, so be warned on this next one!

From a young age, Komin had a thirst for unlimited power and control over others. In addition to the murders he carried out and ordered, he kidnapped and tortured many more. He also became known as The Slaveholder, due to the way he kept his victims in a nine-metre bunker under a garage on his property.

At various intervals over a two-year period, he had six slaves chained up in the dungeon. For the slaves under his control, it was pure terror, but for Komin, it was the fulfilment of a dream he'd had since he was a teenager.

Creation of the factory

The maniac had come from a poor background, born in 1950s Russia to a broken family of war-torn survivors and industrial workers. It was rumoured that he was left alone most of the time. At the age of 18, he was sentenced to three years in prison for vandalism and hooliganism.

While in prison, he met a fellow convict who had kept homeless people in his basement. The prisoner spoke of how he felt like God and had unlimited power and control over the people in his basement. Undisturbed by the nature of the man's crimes, Komin realised it was an experience that he wanted for himself.

A few years after being released from prison, he yearned for his own dungeon but knew he couldn't get away with it for too long without being found out. So he came up with the idea of creating his own textile production company. He would be able to create a legitimate business while keeping slaves at the same time.

He roped in some friends to help him build a bunker under his garage that could hold the necessary space to begin the company as a start-up. Suddenly involved with the business community of the town, he was given the funds to get the equipment necessary to start manufacturing.

By 1995, the factory had multiple rooms, electric connections, ventilation, and a makeshift elevator designed to move goods up and down. Except it was to become more than just a workplace, and Komin seemed to be brazen about his plans for the facility.

Slave collection

One room had three bunk beds and an old television set while another had three sewing machines. Three trapdoors separated the bunker from the garage, with one of the doors having been stolen from a military base.

Komin ensured the steel ladder to the bunker was electrified so that his future slaves couldn't escape. He put up pictures of naked women, including hardcore images on the walls, to add to the bizarreness of the set-up, so that his slaves knew what to do.

In early 1995, Komin met Vera Talpayeva outside of a school and lured her back to the garage on the promise of easy money. Instead, he drugged her with clonidine laced vodka, and she garnered the unfortunate label of becoming his first slave and prisoner.

His next catch was a young tailor named Tatyana Melnikova who he lured back to his bunker. On the way back, they bumped into his first slave's boyfriend, Nikolai Malykh. Nikolai began asking the whereabouts of his girlfriend, and Komin gladly said he would show him. He took Tatyana and Nikolai back to the bunker where he drugged them both.

He decided he didn't want a man as a slave, and so after a couple of days, he poisoned Nikolai and knocked him out. He ordered the two female slaves to strip Nikolai of all his clothes. Komin then drove him to a remote field and watched as he died of exposure in the cold Winter weather.

One week later, his body was discovered. It was suspected to have been an unfortunate accident at the time. Nikolai's clothes were alleged to have been rethreaded and resold to unknowing market sellers.

The maniac evolves

Now with two slaves in his bunker, he abused and raped both of them as and when he wanted. But his passion for keeping slaves grew and he wanted more workers for his business. Tatyana was the better tailor and put together various types of clothing that Komin would sell to other businesses, and at markets.

At the same time, he wanted to extend the bunker and fill it with more slaves. When his first victim, Vera, proved unable to carry out the structural works, he went looking for another victim.

Komin lured 37-year-old alcoholic Yevgeny Shishov to the bunker on the promise of more drink and easy paid work. A few days later, upon realising that Shishov was an electrician, Komin decided to kill him in case he worked out how to turn off the electrical current and escape through the doors.

If what Komin had done to that point was horrific enough, what he did next was simply barbaric. He created a makeshift electric chair purely to execute Shishov. He tied Shishov to the chair naked and secured him with exposed electric wires attached to his nipples, testicles, neck, face and stomach. He then ordered the two female slaves to push the two switches.

Shishov was barbarically electrocuted in front of them and his body was later removed and buried in the forest. Komin decided that because Vera was now an accomplice to murder, he knew she could be trusted. Komin convinced his slaves they were accessories to murder, and they fell under his barbaric spell.

Komin released Vera out into the open for the sole purpose of finding him a new prisoner. She had her back against a wall and followed Komin's orders to the letter. She brought another female back to the bunker named Tatiana Kozikova, a young local girl desperate for work. Komin then ordered the three of them to work 18 hours a day, creating dressing gowns and shorts for the business – which was doing rather well in the outside world.

Torture and more slaves

The two latter prisoners suddenly decided to escape one day and managed to force Komin into one of the rooms where they jammed the door shut. But Komin wasn't trapped for long and he got himself out and dragged his slaves back before they had a chance to free themselves from the bunker.

For trying to escape, Komin gave the pair a choice of punishments; have their mouths cut to their ears or have the word slave tattooed on their foreheads. They both chose the tattoo over the slashing. From then on, Komin would regularly beat and rape his slaves to keep them under control. He had them wear collars and shackles and chained them to the wall.

A few months later, Vera was sent out to get another slave but she disappeared, deciding to runaway instead – much to Komin's annoyance. Though he had no concerns that she would let the world know what was going on in his bunker, she was an accessory to murder after all.

Komin then lured 27-year-old homeless person Tatyana Nazimova, giving himself three slaves with a similar forename, not that their names had mattered by that point. She jumped at the chance of being fed with a roof over her head. Komin then discovered that she was mentally and physically disabled, so he decided to only use her for sexual purposes.

Over the following year, the conditions in the bunker were becoming atrocious and disgusting. The prisoners begged Komin to give them more food, as he starved them on regular occasions. He responded by saying that if they wanted more food then he would cut up the body of a dead slave and feed it to them.

A year passed and Komin had become bored with his most recent sex slave and starved her for almost a week before injecting her with brake fluid. She died instantly. He put her corpse on a sled, drove to a nearby field and dumped her body in the open.

In January 1997, Komin's first victim, Vera, bumped into him while he was out looking for a new slave. Reports showed they chatted away like old friends. Astonishingly, Vera agreed to financial and sexual rewards for finding him new markets to sell at – and more slaves.

He got her on board by telling her that she had pressed the switch that killed Shishov in the electric chair. Two days later, Vera lured 22-year-old Irina Ganyushkina to the bunker, where she was drugged and added to his collection of slaves.

Forced to live on

Komin attempted to fertilise Irina with injections in order to grow an army of slaves he could control. He had a vision that if Irina and any newer slaves were capable of giving birth then he wouldn't have to lure slaves anymore, he could create them.

At the same time, he decided to punish Vera for running away in the first instance. He tortured and beat her for half a day before giving her a choice of drinking antifreeze or having it injected into her. She chose to drink it and he made the other slaves watch her ordeal before she horrifically died of her injuries.

In what can only be described as a twisted twist, Komin claimed he fell in love with his latest prisoner, Irina, and wanted to marry her. The remaining two slaves, Tatyana and Tatiana suddenly saw an opportunity to escape and begged Irina to agree to the marriage.

In the Summer of 1997, Komin took Irina to his apartment to prepare for the wedding but she escaped and ran to the police. Komin was arrested shortly after. A friend of Komin's, Mikheyev, was arrested as an accomplice for helping him build the bunker in the first place, along with the knowledge that he knew what Komin was doing.

The two remaining slaves were rescued from the bunker. They had been underground for two years and had to wear a special bandage around their eyes, so their eyesight wouldn't be damaged by the light.

In 1999, Komin was sentenced to life imprisonment for four murders and various slave trade charges. Mikheyev was given 20 years in prison. Four days later, Komin killed himself by cutting the iliac artery at the base of his abdomen. He bled out before he could be saved.

When the two remaining victims had a fundraiser set up for them to remove the tattoos on their heads, not one person donated. In fact, the Russian public blamed the victims for their ordeal claiming that real women would have either died or killed their captor.

Many saw the victims as having brought it upon themselves, which later caused uproar when their story was published in the New York Times. Komin's story remains one of Russia's most disturbing crimes.

Fortunately, the maniac was caught before realising his full vision of an army of slaves. Unfortunately, he got away with it for so long. We can only begin to imagine the unwritten horrors that his slaves were subjected to – and the horrors he had planned for them next.

Great Santa Claus Robbery

The day before Christmas Eve in 1927, Santa Claus and his gang walked into a bank in Texas and robbed the joint!

On 23rd December 1927, the thriving city of Cisco, Texas was home to over 15,000 residents. It had become an oil and gas boomtown, bringing industry and business to the area. In fact, Texas in 1927 was doing really well! Well enough to attract a swarm of bank robbers to the State.

Bank robbing was such a common occurrence, due to the amount of cash the banks had, that there were on average three to four banks being robbed every single day. The epidemic forced the Texas Banker's Association to offer a reward of $5,000 to any citizen brave enough to shoot a bank robber.

Already with a price on their heads, Marshall Ratliff and his gang of robbers, charged into the National Bank of Cisco, with Ratliff dressed as Santa. Who was ever going to shoot poor Santa Clause?

A genius plan

Ratliff was a well-known Cisco native, who was born in the city, only to fall into a life of crime. He had already been convicted of bank robbery a couple of years earlier and served time in Texas for robbing a bank in Valera. He was unusually pardoned by Texas Governor Ma Ferguson, who released him only a year into his long sentence.

As the Christmas holidays drew close, Ratliff became tempted by the amount of money that was heading into the banks. But he knew that he would be recognised wherever he went, so he came up with what he thought was a genius plan.

He was going to rob the bank with his brother, Lee Ratliff, but Lee was arrested shortly before the robbery. He roped in fellow convicts Henry Helms and Robert Hill, who he had spent time in prison with.

They too, were tempted by a potentially big haul which meant they could buy gifts for their families at Christmas. Rounding off the gang was Louis Davis, a relative of Helms who had become increasingly desperate due to a growing family and lack of finances.

One night, as they sat around planning the robbery, Ratliff hit them with the best idea he'd ever had. They would rob the bank dressed as Santa Claus. No one would suspect a bank robber dressed as Santa Claus during the Christmas holidays, and because many people dressed as Santa at that time of year, they would be difficult to track down.

The idea, if it had worked, would have seen them make off with a substantial sum of money. Except, the Santa robbery, at least for the gang, was to go horribly wrong. In the end, to hide his identity, only Ratliff dressed as Santa as the others thought it to be a preposterous ideas.

A failed plan

In the late morning on the 23rd, Ratliff borrowed a Santa suit from a boarding house owner and set the plan into action. The other three dropped him off many blocks from the bank where he walked through Cisco dressed as Santa Claus. He got so into his role that he was seen talking to children and skipping with them down the street.

Then he walked into the National Bank where he was greeted by bank workers and customers. Thrilled to see Santa so close to Christmas, many customers called out, 'hello Santa!' But Santa was an evil Santa.

The Christmas cheer of the bank suddenly fell apart and turned nasty when the other three unmasked bank robbers marched in behind Santa and pointed their guns at the bank workers. They shouted at the customers to lay down on the ground.

Still disguised as Santa, Ratliff pushed through the security gate and took the bank pistol from under the desk. He then forced a bank worker to open the safe and fill the sack he was carrying with cash. By the time Santa's sack was full, they had over $12,000 in cash and $150,000 in security bonds.

While the robbery was taking place, a woman and her daughter were passing the bank when they say Santa inside. The little girl asked her mother if she could pop inside to see Santa. The mother obliged and walked into the bank to see Santa holding a gun and shouting at people to stay down. Shocked, they ran out of the bank shouting that a robbery was taking place.

Before Santa and his posse knew what was going on, armed residents of Cisco, along with police had surrounded the bank. A large scale shoot-out occurred between the robbers and citizens of Cisco. The four robbers took two young girls' hostage and managed to escape the scene, but Helms shot dead Chief of Police Bit Bedford and officer George Carmichael.

Ratliff and Davis were injured during the shoot-out but still managed to get away. Except the car they chose to escape in had a flat tyre and no gas. During the confusion, as they looked for another car, Davis was left in the car with the flat tyre, where he died of his gunshot wound. The other three managed to escape in another car with the money.

What followed was one of the strangest manhunts in American history.

Santa fugitive

Ratliff, Hill, and Helms dropped the two little girls on the side of the road and led police and civilians on a three day State-wide manhunt. The robbery had become such big news that the police were forced to put out a picture of the robber. As they didn't yet know who was behind the Santa mask, they put out a picture of – you guessed it – Santa Claus.

The picture of Santa was circulated in the press, and suddenly, the city of Cisco made the national news. Over the Christmas period, many newspapers ran with the Santa robbery story, including the image of Santa that the Cisco police had sent out, on the cover of the papers.

The townsfolk and police chased down the robbers in cars, on horseback, and by foot, scouring the local areas, leaving no stone unturned. At a Mass on Christmas Day, when a visiting Christian Santa entered the church, a little boy was heard crying and said; *Santa, why did you rob the bank*?

Three days after the daring robbery, all three men were captured and the money and bonds returned to the National Bank. Helms was sentenced to death for the shooting deaths of Bedford and Carmichael. He was executed shortly after. Hill was sentenced to jail time and was the only robber to survive past the trial, he was eventually released and died of old age.

But the most gruesome fate was saved for Santa. At his trial, Ratliff, who had suffered six gunshot wounds, claimed he was mentally ill and requested he be found not guilty by reason of insanity. The judge refused the plea outright. While he was awaiting trial, Ratliff managed to break out of his cell, and took a gun from the desk drawer of the Eastland County Jail.

He shot and killed one of the jail guards, Tom Jones, and escaped from the jail but he didn't get far. Upon hearing what Ratliff had done, the citizens of Cisco went on a hunting mission, hellbent on serving their own brand of justice.

A lynch mob managed to track down Ratliff and they hung him from a wire between two telephone poles. His body was on display for an entire night and day. After the dust had settled on Cisco's bizarre Christmas, six people were dead, including three of the robbers, and eight others had been seriously injured.

In 1967, a memorial to the daring robbery was placed on the side of the building that housed the bank. The bank that Santa robbed became a historic Texas landmark. The real Santa's reputation was undamaged by the events.

The Fateful Story of Treaty Oak

We look at the bizarre tale of an occultist who attempted to kill a 600-year-old victim, a tree called Treaty Oak, that owned its own land.

In the 16th Century, in Texas, Comanche, Tonkawa, and Tejas Indian tribes would gather together at a grove of 14 trees they considered sacred. They called the location, the Council Oaks, and it was a place where they would discuss the launching of war and peace parties.

The trees were considered so sacred that the females of the tribe would concoct a special tea made from honey and the acorns of the oak. This, they believed, would protect their men in battle and honour the sacred ground on which the trees grew.

In the early 19th Century, many decades after the British and Europeans had invaded the Americas, a Texas pioneer met with the local tribes to strike a peace treaty. Stephen Austin called a tense meeting with the Indians at their sacred ground within the grove of ancient trees.

Between them, they negotiated and signed the first boundary treaty of Texas, following the deaths of some local children. By 1927, just one of the trees remained standing, a 600-year-old tree that was given the name of the Treaty Oak.

At around the same time, the American Forestry Association travelled to the grove and declared the Treaty Oak one of the finest examples of oak tree in the world. Soon after, the landowners who had come to claim the land the tree was on, couldn't afford to pay property taxes.

In 1937, the City of Austin purchased the land from them and secured the future of the Treaty Oak, proclaiming the park the tree was in, was now owned by the tree itself.

Until 1989 when an occultist named Paul Cullen decided to cast a spell and poison the tree with a powerful herbicide.

Poisoning of Treaty Oak

By the late 1980s, the tree's branches had an incredible spread of over 125 feet. Imagine the Sleepy Hollow tree but ten-fold, the tree was huge, so big that it had become a protected site. John Giedraitis was one of Austin's first city foresters, and he was accustomed with many of the parks and trees, specifically Treaty Oak.

He claimed you only had to stand near the Treaty Oak, to realise the Native Indians had been correct, that it was sacred ground, and more so, a sacred tree. John believed this so much that he even proposed to his future wife under the branches of the tree.

One day, in the Summer of 1989, John was hosting foresters from other cities and took them on a ground tour of the parks he looked after. As they neared the Treaty Oak, the headliner of the tour, they all noticed the grass was dying around it.

When John investigated the dying grass, he noticed that the leaves of the Treaty Oak were fading, which was unusual for the Summer months. Yet, John knew his role well and realised that due to the discolouration and deterioration of the leaves and branches, he suspected the tree had been subject to chemical poisoning.

Armed with that knowledge, he enlisted local foresters to dig up some of the soil and get it sent off to University laboratories to see what was going on. One week later, the results came back. Treaty Oak was being poisoned by a powerful chemical and herbicide known under the trade name of Velpar, sold by a company called DuPont.

The results of the soil test confirmed to John what he feared the most, the tree had been intentionally poisoned, and had been specifically targeted for the attack. Before he knew it, the story of the poisoning of Treaty Oak had made headline news, not just in Austin, but across the world.

International tree-saving effort

The poisoning of Treaty Oak reached the front pages of National Geographic, Time Magazine, People Magazine, and newspaper headlines in many countries. Despite the outpouring of grief and shock, the local police department thought the whole thing was a joke and put it down to criminal mischief, not worth investigating.

Except, the international community had other ideas.

American businessman and billionaire, Henry Perot, heard about the story, and was touched by the amount of people that wanted to help save the tree. He reached out to the forestry department of Austin and told them to do whatever was needed to save the tree, and he would put up all the finances for the efforts and for the resulting investigation.

Overwhelmed with the attention of the world, and a blank cheque from one of America's richest men, John called in the country's tree experts and scientists to rescue Treaty Oak. Who all said that the tree would not survive and would be completely dead in a matter of months.

While they did everything possible, including injecting the tree with salt and sugar, using fresh spring water, and protecting it from the Summer Sun, an undercover cop began searching for the culprit.

Spell for a broken heart

After over a decade of working undercover, John Jones was now a detective, and was given the Treaty Oak case as his first unit job. Other officers constantly mocked him as the victim was a tree, but Jones was taken aback with the international outcry, even taking calls from England and Japan, begging him to find the culprit.

Though there was no hard evidence to go by, Jones tracked down a woman named Cindy Blanco who had called the office claiming she knew who the poisoner was. She would sometimes carpool with a man named Paul Cullen, a community mental health patient, who would always talk about witchcraft and spells.

Apparently he was in love with his mental health therapist but she hadn't returned his love and he was looking to black magic for a way to mend his broken heart. He had told Cindy that he needed to kill a large living thing so that when it decomposed, his love for his therapist would also vanish.

Jones decided to put Cindy undercover to get a confession from Cullen and she agreed to it. Based on the confession she got from Cullen, Jones was able to get a warrant for Cullen's residence in Austin. They discovered books on occultism, witchcraft, alternative religions, and more importantly – soil samples that tested positive for Velpar.

Symbol of survival

Cullen was arrested and sent to trial where he was ultimately convicted of criminal mischief and sentenced to nine years in prison. The world could breathe again but Treaty Oak still needed saving.

As the weeks went by, thousands of people descended on Treaty Oak's park, and left offerings to the tree and the sacred ground on which it sat. The location was visited by new age travellers, wiccans, and even Buddhist monks, who hoped to connect with the tree's spirit.

People left money, food, drink and letters. The detective unit at the Austin Police Department were even receiving 'get well soon' cards from all over the world. As the following Spring came around, Treaty Oak showed signs of recovery and miraculously began growing again.

Though it still bears the scars of its attack, the Treaty Oak still stands strong in the City of Austin and never stopped growing. Eight years after the attack, the tree produced it first crop of acorns, a testament to the tree's strength and hardiness.

John was blown away by the amount of people and worshippers who turned up to help the tree, and claimed it to be a powerful life force, an ancient sacred area, and a symbol of survival.

Treaty Oak still owns the land it grows on.

Bonus material

The Orange Sunshine Acid

With most violent crime, be it serial killing, terrorist attacks or war crimes, there will be the conspiracies. One of the biggest involved the Central Intelligence Agency's Project MK Ultra and the Orange Sunshine Acid.

From 1953 until an estimated 1973, the CIA carried out hundreds of secret experiments on willing and unwilling U.S. citizens. The initial aim was to test and gain data on the use of hallucinogens such as LSD which were starting to become popular with the hippy crowd within the States at the time.

This along with other similar drugs were tested for information gathering and possible psychological torture effects. The public were made aware of the illicit project in 1975. It was only through a congressional investigation into illegal CIA activities that the project was uncovered.

So how deep did MK-Ultra affect the people they secretly tested on?

The Charles Manson effect

The aim of MK-Ultra was to control a human's behaviour with drugs, hallucinogens, or other various psychological methods. It was said that 150 people were tested on. Sometimes people knew they were participating in a study but many had no idea. The testing involved drugs, hallucinogens and electroshock therapy.

Many tests were carried out in universities, hospitals or on criminals in prisons. Typically, as with all these things, the CIA destroyed most MK-Ultra data when the program came to an end in 1973.

The most famous to be linked to the project were Charles Manson and the Manson Family, who kickstarted the 1970s with their bloody rampage. Manson himself used mind-control techniques, along with hypnotism and LSD to turn well-to-do women and men into killing machines.

He was a part of the hippie movement at the time when MK-Ultra was active. A new strain of LSD, called Orange Sunshine was being used by the killers just before they took part in the infamous Tate-LaBianca murders.

One of the Family members, 'Tex' Watson, wrote in his memoir that it was Orange Sunshine LSD that found him believing in Manson's violent visions. He said it was a hitherto unknown strain of LSD and that it was a mentally powerful acid that '*drew stuff out of your mind*'.

It was claimed the CIA's prime objective was to debunk the hippie movement and make it look bad. The movement itself was becoming an economical and sociological threat to both the government, its leaders, and the Vietnam Conflict.

The CIA needed a way of showing the American people that flower power was actually controlled by Satanists and the hippie movement was evil. Thus, they needed to conduct a massive covert operation, to convince the American public that hippies were in fact the biggest evil to face the United States since the Nazis.

The Brotherhood of Eternal Love

Orange Sunshine LSD was created and sold by a group going by the name of The Brotherhood of Eternal Love. They operated at a Los Angeles beach resort. One of its dealers, Ronald Stark, had known connections to the CIA.

The same batch of Orange Sunshine LSD was available all too easily, four months later, at a free concert held at Altamont Speedway. Four people died at what should have been a peaceful festival. One of them was stabbed to death by a group who had taken multiple tabs of Orange Sunshine.

Some of the attendees at the concert who were familiar with recreational hallucinogens claimed afterwards the Orange Sunshine acid felt different and that it was contaminated.

It would give them negative emotions and feelings of wanting to be violent and cause harm to others. In some instances it felt like they just wanted to kill someone. Shockingly, Orange Sunshine was in use during the Vietnam War and we know what happened out there.

Charles Manson was serving a prison sentence in Vacaville Prison, a facility that was known to be used by the CIA for its MK-Ultra program. The theory is that Manson was a mind-controlled visionary set loose by the CIA.

"I'm only what I've been trained to be. Jimmy Carter made me what I am." – Charles Manson.

Operation Midnight Climax

And then there was Operation Midnight Climax! Can you believe what they got away with all those years ago? Operation Midnight Climax was a branch of MK-Ultra in which the CIA employed prostitutes to lure punters to CIA safe houses. Once there, drug experiments would take place, unbeknownst to the victim.

The CIA dosed the men with LSD and watched the effects on the men's behaviour. Amazingly, the CIA had free-reign over the experiments and even had cocktail parties as they watched the punter and prostitute from behind a two-way-mirror in the buildings. Midnight Climax tests were carried out in San Francisco, New York, and California.

Ken Kesey

The author of One Flew Over the Cuckoo's Nest volunteered for the MK-Ultra experiments with LSD. He would subsequently go on to hold LSD parties that he referred to as Acid Tests.

The Unabomber, Ted Kaczynski

Kaczynski began his bombing campaign in 1978 and had previously volunteered for the MK-Ultra LSD experiments.

James 'Whitey' Bulger

The notorious Boston mob leader, who killed 19 people, volunteered for MK-Ultra in 1956 while in prison in order to reduce his sentence. He said the LSD took him to 'the depths of insanity'.

Both Charles Manson and Whitey Bulger became more violent after their short prison sentences. This would potentially have been after MK-Ultra participation, unwittingly or willingly. However, the remaining evidence is thin as it has been mostly wiped from history.

We'll never truly know if some serial killers and crime incidents were a result of the MK-Ultra program. But we've both learned enough in this book to know that anything is possible, no matter how dark it might be.

Bitesize Extras

Fainting Epidemic

In West Bank, in 1983, a fainting epidemic began and carried on for many months. Large numbers of female Palestinians complained of fainting and dizziness. Many were teenage girls, with a small number of female Israeli soldiers in multiple West Bank towns. Over the course of the epidemic, at least 943 people had been hospitalised.

Palestinian leaders accused Israeli settlers and officials of using biological warfare in West Bank schools to drive Arabs out of the area. However, the truth was far more bizarre.

On March 31st, the Permanent Representative to the UN from Iraq asked the United Nations Security Council to look into the possibility that almost 1,000 Palestinian schoolgirls were being poisoned.

Less than a week later, the Security Council formally requested the Secretary General of the UN to conduct an independent investigation of the poisoning. A large investigation discovered no organic cause of the fainting and believed mass hysteria to be the most likely cause of the epidemic.

Their findings were backed up by the International Red Cross and the World Health Organisation. Later in April, a team of US medical researchers concluded the fainting outbreaks were caused by mass psychological illness which was labelled as anxiety.

Human vs. particle accelerator

In 1978, Russian scientist, Anatoli Petrovich Bugorski was a researcher who worked with the largest Soviet particle accelerator, the U-70 Synchrotron. Bugorski was checking a piece of equipment when the safety mechanisms failed and he ended up sticking his head into the path of a fully powered proton beam travelling at the speed of light.

Bugorski's face swelled up beyond recognition and his skin started to peel which revealed the path the beam had taken through his head. Bugorski miraculously went on to survive but his left side was paralysed and he suffered ongoing seizures.

Despite the failing of the safety measures, no one was held to account and the Russian Government put a lid on the incident for over a decade.

Squirrel shuts down the stock exchange

In December 1987, a squirrel burrowed through a telephone line and shut down the entire Nasdaq Stock Exchange. A nutty bushy-tailed rodent chewed through a cable and cut power to the town of Trumbull, where the Nasdaq's main trading systems were located at the time.

And it wouldn't be the last time! In 1994, those pesky nut-hoarding tree-climbers did it again and shut the Nasdaq for over half an hour. Clearly, the squirrel population of Trumbull took offence to the stock markets being in their town.

Cold Case Files '78-'81

OUT NOW!

Bibliography

A selected bibliography and resource.

BBC Coventry & Warwickshire. (2014) *"Uncovering Warwickshire's sinister secret."* BBC.

Bean, Matt. (2003). *"Matrix makes its way into courtrooms as defence strategy."* CNN International Edition.

Black, Arthur. (1982) *"Marriage and the bigamist."* Nipigon Gazette.
http://images.ourontario.ca/Partners/Nipigon/NPL002288384p f_0004.pdf

Clark, Laura. (2015) *"Grave robbers once held Charlie Chaplin's body for ransom."* Smithsonian Magazine.

Court of Appeals of Indiana. (1980) *"Roberts v. Wabash Life Ins. Co."* 410 N.E.2d 1377 (Ind. Ct. App. 1980)

Dhruv Bose, Swapnil. (2019) *"True story of how Charlie Chaplin's coffin and body were stolen in an extortion plot."* Far Out Magazine.

Durante, Thomas. (2012) *"Killer behind headless body in topless bar headline hoping to go free after 30 years behind bars."* Daily Mail.

Eccleston, Ben. (2017) *"Gory Valentine's Day murder remains oldest unsolved killing in Warwickshire."* Coventry Live.

Famous Trees of Texas. *"Treaty Oak"*. Texas A&M University.

Glass, Ira. Et al. (2008) *"The ghost of Bobby Dunbar."* Transcript from This American Life.

Graham, Cork. (2011) *"The Bamboo Chest 2nd Edition: An Adventure in Healing the Trauma of War."* ISBN: 978-0970358059. Rigel Media.

Greene, A. C. (1999). *"The Santa Claus Bank Robbery."* ISBN 978-1574410716. Texas A&M University Press.

Hardwick, Courtney. (2021) *"Queer Crime: The Double Life of Herb Baumeister."* In Magazine.

Henderson, Chris. (2019) *"Blue Jays obscure memories: Dave Winfield accidentally kills a bird."* Jays Journal.

Higgins, Will. (2012) *"House with dark past fulfils family dream."* Chillicothe Gazette. www.newspapers.com/clip/21146336/chillicothe-gazette.

History.com. (2009) *"Grave robbers steal Charlie Chaplin's body."* History Channel.

Holder, Bev. (2018) *"Bella experts to mark 75th anniversary of unsolved Hagley murder."*

Jerome, Richard. (1996) *"While Julie Was Away."* People Magazine.

Jolly, Nathan. (2019) *"How severed arm regurgitated by tiger shark led to murder mystery."* Nationwide News Limited.

Lowe, Sam. (2012) *"Giovanni Vigliotto: A conman with 105 wives."* Arizona Oddities.

New York Times. (1978) *"Actress is Slain at Michigan Audition."* New York Times. https://www.nytimes.com/1978/04/11/archives/actress-is-slain-at-michigan-audition.html

New York Times. (1978) *"Sentencing set for Michigan man in Hammer slaying of woman."* New York Times.
https://www.nytimes.com/1978/06/17/archives/sentencing-set-for-michigan-man-in-hammer-slaying-of-woman.html

New York Times. (1983) *"Tale of man and 105 wives' packs courtroom."* New York Times National.
https://www.nytimes.com/1983/02/06/us/tale-of-man-and-105-wives-packs-courtroom.html

Schram, Jamie. (2012) *"Headless body in topless bar killer seeks release from prison."* New York Post.

Slife, Erika. (2009) *"Most of my memories are from behind four walls."* Chicago Tribune.
https://www.chicagotribune.com/news/ct-xpm-2009-05-06-0905040322-story.html

Smith, Justin. (2019) *"The time Charlie Chaplin's corpse went missing."* Little White Lies.

Terre Haute Tribune. (1975) *"Mystery man probed by grand Jury."* Terre Haute Tribune.

Truth News. (1935). *"What sick shark revealed."* Truth Newspaper Melbourne.
https://trove.nla.gov.au/newspaper/article/169353866

Look for more in the Bizarre True Crime Series from Ben Oakley & Twelvetrees Camden

OUT NOW!

Printed in Great Britain
by Amazon

87813261R00102